Slimming Magazine was first published in 1969 and now has a readership of one and a quarter million. Year by year, *Slimming Magazine*'s reputation has grown as the world's leader in its field. This success is based on one editorial aim: to be the best friend a dieter ever had ... a friend who is understanding, honest, sensible – and fun. And supremely well informed. *Slimming Magazine* is able to advise on diet and nutrition with all the authority of an internationally respected scientific team. Its very human experts also have an unrivalled insight in the everyday practical problems of dieting: they have suffered themselves!

Glynis McGuinness was senior home economist on *Slimming Magazine* for four years. She previously managed the executive directors' dining room at Thames TV, spent two years working in a special diets department of a hospital in Sydney, Australia and has worked as a home economist for Metal Box and Lyons Maid. She edits a number of *Slimming Magazine* booklets each year.

Sybil Greatbatch is deputy editor of *Slimming Magazine*. Before joining the magazine in 1978, she worked full time as an editor for BBC Publications while running a *Slimming Magazine Club* in her spare time. She has also edited *The Complete Dieting Revolution* (1981) and *Slimming: the Complete Guide* (1982).

Slimming Magazine's

Working Girl's Diet Book

edited by Glynis McGuinness
and Sybil Greatbatch

Fontana Paperbacks

First published by Fontana Paperbacks 1983

Set in 10 on 11pt Linotron Plantin
Made and printed in Great Britain by
William Collins Sons & Co. Ltd, Glasgow

Contents

Introduction

If you are a working girl you probably won't want to spend a long time preparing meals in the evening. You'll want a lunch that you can take to work, and you'll need to breakfast in a hurry. In this book we have selected recipes and menus that will allow you to do all this and diet just as fast as you like.

As a working girl you have one big advantage over a housewife. That is you don't usually have access to the kitchen for a large part of the day. Learn to take advantage of this and try to keep your breakfasts and lunches positively saintly, saving most of your calories for the evening when you may be more tempted to pop into the kitchen to nibble at whatever's available. Of course, there may be days when you want to eat out with friends at lunchtime or in the evening and we have included a chapter on eating out and devised some low-calorie diet savers that you can cook up for your other meal. We've taken care of sweet-toothed dieters also, with a selection of delicious easy-to-make desserts and sweet treats. And if you really cannot manage to diet without nibbling we have devised some very low-calorie little snacks to get you through the day.

Most women and all men will lose weight if they keep to 1500 calories a day. Exactly how fast you lose the pounds will depend on how heavy you weigh, how active you are and your basic metabolism. Very overweight women will lose weight faster than slimmer dieting women on the same number of calories because they need more calories to move their body around. That is why we recommend that if you have more than three stone to lose, you start with 1500 calories a day. If you have between one and three stone to lose, we recommend cutting your calories to 1250 a day. The last few pounds are always the most difficult to shift so when you only have a stone to lose you will need to keep to a strict 1000 calories a day. The more active you are during the diet, the quicker the pounds will disappear. Even if you hate the idea of taking up exercise, you can burn up more calories just by moving about a lot more. Slimming is simply a matter of burning up more calories than you eat so that your body has to draw on its store of fat. If you have a job where you sit down for most of the day, make sure you take a walk at lunchtime and never take a lift when you can walk up a flight of stairs.

Before you start your diet, read the simple rules that follow.

How to use this book

1. On page 11 is a chart showing what you should weigh for your height. The first step is to decide how much weight you have to lose. While you are dieting weigh yourself once a week at about the same time of day and wearing the same clothes to get an accurate account of your weight loss.

2. If you have more than three stone to lose, choose 1500-calorie menus; if you have between one and three stone to lose, choose 1250-calorie menus; if you have one stone or less to lose, choose 1000-calorie menus.

3. It is best to shop for your week's diet in advance if you can. So make a list of the foods you will need. You may repeat a menu as many times as you like but try to incorporate seven different menus into your diet during one month. This will ensure that you get a good balance of all the nutrients you need.

4. Most of the menus include a milk allowance which is included in the total calories. You can also drink freely black tea, black coffee, water and drinks labelled 'low-calorie'. Any other drinks (see list on page 152) must be added on to your calories for the day. If you feel you want to spend 250 calories on alcoholic drinks, for example, choose a 1000-calorie menu and together with the drinks your total for the day will be 1250.

5. Never shop on an empty stomach. You may be tempted to fill your basket with items you didn't really intend to

buy if you feel hungry and deprived. Stick to the list of foods you need for your diet.

6. You are now ready to start your diet. Follow any of our recommended menus carefully – weighing and measuring accurately – and you will lose weight.

7. When you have the idea, you can devise some menus of your own using our recipes and the calorie charts at the back of this book. Follow the basic rule of good nutrition to keep meals varied and include some vegetables, fruit, meat/fish/cheese and cereal each day.

IDEAL WEIGHT CHART Here we provide a guide to your ideal weight – your proper poundage could be up to 7 lb either side of the medium-frame figure given for your height. Your mirror is the best judge of whether you have reached your ideal target weight. You are aiming at a covering that looks good and feels non-flabby.

What a Woman should weigh
without shoes, allowing 2 to 3 lb (or about 1kg) for light indoor clothing

Height			Medium Frame
4-ft-10	1.47m	7-st-8	48kg
4-ft-11	1.50m	7-st-11	49.5kg
5-ft-0	1.52m	8-st-0	51kg
5-ft-1	1.55m	8-st-3	52.5kg
5-ft-2	1.57m	8-st-7	54kg
5-ft-3	1.60m	8-st-9	55kg
5-ft-4	1.63m	8-st-12	56.5kg
5-ft-5	1.65m	9-st-1	57.5kg
5-ft-6	1.68m	9-st-8	61kg
5-ft-7	1.70m	9-st-9	61.5kg
5-ft-8	1.73m	9-st-12	62.5kg
5-ft-9	1.75m	10-st-2	64.5kg
5-ft-10	1.78m	10-st-5	66kg
5-ft-11	1.80m	10-st-10	68kg
6-ft-0	1.83m	11-st-0	70kg

What a Man should weigh
without shoes, allowing 2 to 3 lb (or about 1kg) for light indoor clothing.

Height			Medium Frame
5-ft-1	1.55m	8-st-11	56kg
5-ft-2	1.57m	9-st-1	57.5kg
5-ft-3	1.60m	9-st-4	59kg
5-ft-4	1.63m	9-st-7	60.5kg
5-ft-5	1.65m	9-st-10	62kg
5-ft-6	1.68m	10-st-1	64kg
5-ft-7	1.70m	10-st-5	66kg
5-ft-8	1.73m	10-st-9	67.5kg
5-ft-9	1.75m	10-st-13	69.5kg
5-ft-10	1.78m	11-st-4	72kg
5-ft-11	1.80m	11-st-8	73.5kg
6-ft-0	1.83m	11-st-12	75.5kg
6-ft-1	1.85m	12-st-3	77.5kg
6-ft-2	1.88m	12-st-8	80kg
6-ft-3	1.90m	13-st-0	82.5kg

Breakfasts for Girls in a Hurry

No working girl we have ever spoken to gets out of bed hours before she has to leave and has a leisurely breakfast. We have devised all the following breakfasts, therefore, so that they can be made in super-quick time.

Cereals make ideal breakfasts for working women. A large packet of cereal will keep for a long time, so you do not have to shop every day, nor even have to think about what you are going to eat. Cereals also provide fibre and a selection of nutrients that are essential for a healthy diet. Remember always to weigh out your cereal, rather than tip it into your dish. Some cereals weigh much lighter than others and guesswork could ruin your calorie calculations.

Bread and crispbread breakfasts are also very simple and quick to make. Again, remember to weigh and measure accurately. Use a standard 5ml measuring spoon and not just any teaspoon from your cutlery drawer. If a recipe requires a level spoonful, take any excess from the top of your spoon with a knife. A level teaspoon measures 5ml, a rounded one 10ml. It is particularly important to be accurate when weighing fats, which are very high in calories. If your kitchen scales do not weigh accurately in small amounts, you can weigh out an ounce of butter or low-fat spread and cut that into four, to give you 7g (1/4 oz) portions.

Skimmed milk has about half the calories of Silver Top. If you do have difficulty getting skimmed you could try mixing Silver Top with the same amount of water. Some people find this mixture quite acceptable when served on cereals. Or use reconstituted dried low-fat milk.

The following breakfasts start at 90 calories and rise to 250 calories.

Tomatoes on Toast
Serves 1: 90 calories

227-g (8-oz) can tomatoes
1 small slice bread, 25g (1 oz)

Put the tomatoes in a small saucepan and heat. Toast the bread and serve the tomatoes on top.

All-Bran
Serves 1: 100 calories

25g (1 oz) All-Bran
75ml (3 fl. oz) skimmed milk
5ml (1 level teaspoon) Hermesetas Sprinkle Sweet,
  optional

Carefully weigh the cereal and serve with hot or cold milk and Sprinkle Sweet, if liked.

Cornflakes *or* Rice Krispies
Serves 1: 105 calories

20g (³⁄₄ oz) cornflakes *or* Rice Krispies
75ml (3 fl. oz) skimmed milk
5ml (1 level teaspoon) Hermesetas Sprinkle Sweet,
  optional

Carefully weigh the cereal and serve with hot or cold milk and Sprinkle Sweet, if liked.

Grapefruit and Marmite Crispbreads
Serves 1: 105 calories

¹⁄₂ grapefruit
2 Energen *or* Ryvita
  crispbreads

7g (¹⁄₄ oz) low-fat spread
Marmite *or* yeast extract

Start with the grapefruit half (you can add a no-calorie liquid artificial sweetener, if you wish). Follow with the crisp-breads, spread with low-fat spread and a little Marmite or yeast extract.

Boiled Egg and Crispbread
Serves 1: 105 calories

1 egg (size 3)
1 Energen *or* Ryvita crispbread

Boil the egg and serve with unbuttered crispbread. If you don't have time to boil an egg in the morning, the egg can be hardboiled the night before. Slice and use to top the crispbread.

Bran Flakes or Special K with Raisins
Serves 1: 130 calories

20g (¾ oz) Kelloggs 30% Bran Flakes *or* Special K
15ml (1 level tablespoon) raisins *or* sultanas
75ml (3 fl. oz) skimmed milk

Carefully weigh the cereal. Mix with dried fruit and serve with hot or cold milk.

All-Bran with Dried Apricots
Serves 1: 140 calories

25g (1 oz) All-Bran
3 dried apricots
125ml (4 fl. oz) skimmed milk

Roughly chop the dried apricots and mix with the cereal. Serve with hot or cold milk.

Poached Egg on Toast
Serves 1: 145 calories

1 egg (size 3)
1 small slice bread, 25g (1 oz)

Poach the egg in lightly salted water and a little vinegar (or in a non-stick poacher). Serve on the toasted bread. Do not add butter or margarine.

Crispbreads with Honey
Serves 1: 150 calories

3 Krispen crispbreads
15g (1/2 oz) low-fat spread
15ml (1 level tablespoon) honey

Cover the crispbread with the carefully weighed low-fat spread and honey.

Marmalade *or* Jam and Toast
Serves 1: 155 calories

2 small slices slimmers' bread
7g (1/4 oz) butter *or* margarine
10ml (2 level teaspoons) marmalade *or* jam

Toast the bread and spread with butter and marmalade or jam.

Cornflakes, Bran Flakes *or* Rice Krispies
Serves 1: 155 calories

25g (1 oz) cornflakes, 30% Bran Flakes *or* Rice Krispies
125ml (4 fl. oz) skimmed milk
5ml (1 level teaspoon) sugar

Carefully weigh the cereal and serve with hot or cold milk. Sprinkle with sugar making sure it is a level teaspoon, not rounded.

Weetabix
Serves 1: 165 calories
2 Weetabix
5ml (1 level teaspoon) sugar
125ml (4 fl. oz) skimmed milk

Serve the Weetabix with hot or cold milk and sprinkle with sugar, making sure you use a level not a rounded teaspoon.

Porridge with Honey
Serves 1: 175 calories

25g (1 oz) Ready Brek *or* Warm Start
150ml (¼ pint) skimmed milk
5ml (1 level teaspoon) honey *or* sugar

Mix the Ready Brek or Warm Start with hot milk and serve with honey or sugar.

Bacon and Tomatoes
Serves 1: 200 calories

3 rashers streaky bacon
2 tomatoes
1 small slice slimmers' bread

Grill the bacon well on a rack to allow the fat to drip away. Grill the tomatoes. Serve bacon and tomatoes with unbuttered bread, toasted if you wish.

Cheese on Toast
Serves 1: 200 calories

2 small slices slimmers' bread
40g (1½ oz) Edam cheese

Toast the bread on one side. Top the other side with cheese and grill until cheese bubbles.

Cereal with Sliced Banana
Serves 1: 205 calories

25g (1 oz) cornflakes, 30% Bran Flakes, Special K *or*
  Weetaflakes
1 small banana
125ml (4 fl. oz) skimmed milk

Peel and slice the banana and mix with the cereal. Serve with hot or cold milk.

Curd Cheese and Marmite Crispbreads
Serves 1: 210 calories

3 Energen *or* Ryvita crispbreads
Marmite *or* yeast extract
75g (3 oz) curd cheese

Spread the crispbreads with a little Marmite or yeast extract and top with curd cheese.

Bacon and Baked Beans
Serves 1: 210 calories

2 rashers streaky bacon
150-g (5.3-oz) can baked beans with tomato sauce

Grill the bacon well on a rack to allow the fat to drip away. Heat the beans and serve with the bacon.

Wholemeal Toast and Marmalade or Honey
Serves 1: 210 calories

2 small slices wholemeal bread, 25g (1 oz) each
15g (½ oz) low-fat spread
10ml (2 level teaspoons) marmalade *or* honey

Toast the wholemeal bread and spread with carefully weighed low-fat spread and marmalade or honey.

Muesli with Apricots
Serves 1: 230 calories

40g (1½ oz) muesli
4 dried apricots *or* 4 apricot halves canned in apple juice
75ml (3 fl. oz) skimmed milk

If you use dried apricots, soak them in water overnight and then drain. Drain the apricots in apple juice. Mix apricot halves with the muesli and serve with skimmed milk.

Scrambled Eggs on Toast
Serves 1: 235 calories

2 eggs (size 3)
30ml (2 tablespoons)
  skimmed milk

salt and pepper
1 small slice bread, 25g
  (1 oz)

Lightly beat the eggs and skimmed milk together and season with salt and pepper. Cook in a non-stick pan over a low heat, stirring all the time, until creamy. While the eggs are cooking, toast the bread. Serve the scrambled eggs on the toast.

Shredded Wheat
Serves 1: 235 calories

2 Shredded Wheat
10ml (2 level teaspoons) sugar
125 ml (4 fl. oz) skimmed milk

Sprinkle Shredded Wheat with sugar and serve with hot or cold milk.

Bacon Sandwich
Serves 1: 240 calories

2 rashers streaky bacon
2 small slices bread, 25g (1 oz) each
10ml (1 rounded teaspoon) tomato ketchup

Grill the bacon well. Use to make a sandwich with the bread and tomato ketchup.

Muesli
Serves 1: 250 calories

50g (2 oz) muesli
125ml (4 fl. oz) skimmed milk

Weigh muesli very carefully and serve with hot or cold milk.

Breakfasts to Take to Work

Some working girls leave home so early in the morning that they prefer not to eat until they get to work. Others just don't fancy breakfast but like to have a snack mid-morning or when the coffee trolley comes round and other colleagues are buying sticky buns and bacon rolls. So we have devised some easy breakfasts to take to work. They can all be prepared the evening before, so there should be no excuse that you didn't have time to bother.

We have also included a list of 'health' bars, chocolate bars, biscuits and crisps which could be bought on the way to work if you find it very difficult to walk past particularly tempting sweet shops and kiosks. A word of warning about chocolate, though. If you are the sort of person who is perfectly happy to eat one small bar in the morning and then forget about chocolate for the rest of the day, fine. But if one bite of a chocolate biscuit or bar gives you the taste for more, and more, and more, best to stay clear of it entirely. Health bars are a good alternative as they are often less sugary than chocolate and have greater filling power.

Calories in this section start at 100 and rise to 290.

Crispbreads with Cheese Spread
Serves 1: 100 calories

2 Cracotte, Crackerbread, Ryvita *or* Vitawheat crispbreads
1 triangle cheese spread

Spread the crispbreads with cheese spread and sandwich together. Wrap in foil or clear food wrap.

Stewed Apple with Sultanas and Yogurt
Serves 1: 105 calories

175g (6 oz) unsweetened stewed apple
15ml (1 level tablespoon) sultanas *or* raisins
30ml (2 level tablespoons) natural yogurt

Mix together the yogurt, apple and sultanas or raisins and take to work in a carton or plastic container.

Yogurt with Wheatgerm and Raisins
Serves 1: 145 calories

1 small carton Dessert Farm Peach and Redcurrant *or* Pear and Banana Yogurt
10ml (1 rounded teaspoon) wheatgerm
15ml (1 level tablespoon) raisins *or* sultanas

Mix together the yogurt, wheatgerm and dried fruit. Take to work in a large yogurt carton, cottage cheese carton or plastic container.

Ham Sandwich
Serves 1: 150 calories

2 small slices slimmers'   mustard, optional
   bread   25g (1 oz) lean cooked ham
7g (¼ oz) low-fat spread

Carefully weigh the low-fat spread and spread onto the bread with a little mustard. Place the ham on bread to make a sandwich.

Yogurt and Muesli
Serves 1: 160 calories

1 small carton natural yogurt
30ml (2 level tablespoons) muesli

Mix together yogurt and muesli and take to work in a large yogurt carton or plastic container.

Egg and Crispbreads
Serves 1: 165 calories

1 egg (size 3)
2 Energen *or* Ryvita
  crispbreads

7g (¼ oz) low-fat spread
5ml (1 level teaspoon)
  Marmite *or* yeast extract

Hard-boil the egg. Spread the crispbreads with low-fat spread and Marmite or yeast extract.

Yogurt and Banana
Serves 1: 205 calories

1 small banana
1 small carton Eden Vale Natural Yogurt with Honey *or* 1
  small carton St Ivel Country Prize Muesli *or* Walnut
  Muesli Yogurt

Slice the banana and mix with the yogurt. Take to work in a large yogurt carton or plastic container.

Banana, Yogurt and Raisins
Serves 1: 210 calories

1 small banana
1 small carton natural
  yogurt
15ml (1 level tablespoon)
  raisins *or* sultanas

15ml (1 level tablespoon)
  wheatgerm

Peel and slice the banana and mix with the yogurt, raisins and wheatgerm. Take to work in a plastic container.

Cottage Cheese and Ham Sandwich
Serves 1: 210 calories

15g (½ oz) lean cooked ham
2 small slices bread, 25g (1 oz) each
50g (2 oz) cottage cheese, plain *or* with chives *or* pineapple

Discard all visible fat from the ham and then chop the lean.
Mix with the cottage cheese and use to make a sandwich with
the two slices of bread.

Citrus Yogurt with Raisins
Serves 1: 215 calories

1 large orange
1 small carton Eden Vale Natural Yogurt with Grapefruit
   or 1 small carton St Ivel Country Prize Grapefruit
   Yogurt
15ml (1 level tablespoon) raisins *or* sultanas

Peel and chop the orange and mix with the yogurt and raisins
or sultanas. Take to work in a large yogurt carton or plastic
container.

Banana and Honey Sandwich
Serves 1: 215 calories

2 small slices bread, 25g (1 oz) each
1 small banana
5ml (1 level teaspoon) honey

Spread one slice of bread with the honey. Peel and mash the
banana and spread over the honey. Top with the other slice
of bread.

Cheese Spread, Tomato and Cucumber Sandwich
Serves 1: 220 calories

2 small slices bread, 25g   1 tomato
  (1 oz) each   few slices cucumber
25g (1 oz) cheese spread
  with onion *or* with chives

Spread the bread with the cheese and make into a sandwich with the sliced tomato and cucumber.

Crispbreads with Liver Sausage and Tomato
Serves 1: 235 calories

50g (2 oz) liver sausage
1 tomato
2 Energen *or* Ryvita crispbreads

Slice the liver sausage and tomato. Wrap all the ingredients separately in clear food wrap and assemble when ready to eat.

Egg and Marmite Sandwich
Serves 1: 275 calories

2 small slices bread, 25g   5ml (1 level teaspoon)
  (1 oz) each   Marmite *or* Bovril
15g (½ oz) low-fat spread   1 egg (size 3), hardboiled

Scrape the bread with the low-fat spread, top with Marmite or Bovril. Slice the egg and make into a sandwich with the bread.

Crunchy 'Health' Bars

If you don't have time to prepare breakfast to take to work, these bars are a fair alternative. Don't buy several at a time, though, with the idea you'll keep one for tomorrow – you won't!

	Calories
Quaker Harvest Crunch Bar	80
Prewett's Fruit and Bran Dessert Bar	85
Prewett's Apple and Date Dessert Bar	95
Prewett's Date and Fig Dessert Bar	110
Prewett's Muesli Fruit Dessert Bar	125
Prewett's Fruit and Nut Dessert Bar	130
Boots Date and Muesli Bar	155
Jordan's Original Crunchy Bar with Honey and Almond	155
Boots Swiss Style Muesli Bar	190

Bought Snacks

If you find sweet and chocolate kiosks and shops hard to resist on your way to work, you could try missing breakfast and allow yourself one of the following instead.

Chocolate Bars and Biscuits

per smallest bar unless otherwise stated

	Calories
Nestle Milky Bar (15g)	80
Rowntree Mackintosh Caramac (16g)	90
Cadbury's Crunchie (20g)	95
McVitie Bandit	95

Rowntree Mackintosh Blue Riband	105
Rowntree Mackintosh Breakaway	105
McVitie Milk Chocolate Sport	105
Rowntree Mackintosh Golden Cup	105
McVitie United	110
Rowntree Mackintosh Kit Kat (2 fingers)	110
Mars Banjo, coconut, single bar	115
Jacobs Club, milk, orange, mint	115
Mars Banjo, peanut, single bar	120
Cadbury's Curly Wurly	130
Jacobs Trio	130
Penguin	130
Mars Twix, single bar	135
Cadbury's Fudge	135
Mars Milky Way	135
Mars Ripple, (26g)	140
Cadbury's Dipped Flake	145
Mars Bounty, plain, per piece	145
Mars Bounty, milk, per piece	150
Rowntree Mackintosh Walnut Whip, plain chocolate, vanilla	165
Cadbury's Crunchie (35g)	165
Rowntree Mackintosh Walnut Whip, milk chocolate, coffee *or* vanilla	170
Cadbury's Border Creme Egg	170
Terry's Milk Chocolate Wafer	175
Terry's Milk Chocolate Orange Wafer	175
Terry's Plain Chocolate Wafer	175
Cadbury's Milk Chocolate Flake (large:34g)	180
Rowntree Mackintosh Texan	180
Rowntree Mackintosh Toffee Crisp, milk	195
Rowntree Mackintosh Aero, peppermint	205
Rowntree Mackintosh Aero, orange	205
Frys Chocolate Cream	210
Cadbury's Dairy Milk Chocolate (40g)	210
Rowntree Mackintosh Aero, milk	210
Rowntree Mackintosh Lion Bar	215

Rowntree Mackintosh Prize	225
Cadbury's Picnic	230
Cadbury's Double Decker	230
Rowntree Mackintosh Drifter	230
Terry's Marzipan Bar	235
Cadbury's Caramel	245
Topic	245
Ovaltine Milk Chocolate (50g)	250
Rowntree Mackintosh Cabana	255
Cadbury's Bournville Chocolate (50g)	260
Rowntree Mackintosh Nutty	260
Nestle Milk Chocolate (50g)	265
Cadbury's Dairy Milk Fruit and Nut (standard)	270
Galaxy Milk Chocolate (50g)	270
Nestle Plain Chocolate (50g)	275
Marathon	310
Mars Bar	325

Crisps and Snacks

per smallest packet

	Calories
KP Sky Divers, any flavour	80
Smiths Chipstiks	105
Golden Wonder Ringos	110
Smiths Frazzles	120
Walkers French Fries	120
Sainsbury's Ready Salted Crisps	125
Burtons Potato Puffs	130
Chipmunk Crisps, all flavours	130
KP Salt and Vinegar Crisps	130
Golden Wonder Crisps, all flavours	135
KP Crisps, any flavour	135
Smiths Crisps *or* Square Crisps	135
KP Ready Salted Mini Chips	135

Tesco Crisps, Ready Salted *or* Salt and Vinegar	135
KP Discos, any flavour	150
Walkers Crisps, all flavours	150
Sainsbury's Cheese Sticks	250

Packed Lunches

When you are dieting it is a good policy to take a packed lunch to work whenever you can. It is almost impossible to calculate calories accurately for meals bought in restaurants, cafes or pubs (more about this in the next chapter).

We carried out an investigation of examples of the most popular sandwiches and rolls that can be bought from sandwich bars, pubs and delicatessens. These ready-made butties ranged from 725 calories for a cheese bap to 365 calories for a plain and simple ham sandwich. The only rolls we found that were suitable to be included in a diet were a tiny egg mayonnaise roll with tomato which was 280 calories, and a salad roll which came to 235 calories.

Here we give recipes for packed lunches which range from 150 calories to 300. All pass our criteria of being very simple to prepare, and some recipes can be made the evening before. You could even buy some of the items on the way to work so there is no need to forget your diet if you forget your lunch.

If you enjoy a sandwich lunch, remember that you can make up your week's supply in advance and freeze them in individual parcels. Salad ingredients and hardboiled eggs, however, do not freeze well.

To accompany your lunch you can have as much black coffee and tea with artificial sweetener as you wish and it will cost you no calories at all. Add one teaspoon of Marvel and it will cost you 5 calories – a level teaspoon of sugar (5ml) will cost 17 calories. For other drinks calories, see page 152.

Cheese and Cucumber Sandwich
Serves 1: 150 calories

2 slices slimmers' bread   few slices cucumber
1 triangle cheese spread   1 medium-sized pear

Make a sandwich with the bread, cheese spread and
cucumber. Wrap and take to work with a pear to be eaten
after your sandwich.

Egg Salad
Serves 1: 150 calories

1 egg (size 3), hardboiled   salt and pepper
50g (2 oz) cucumber
50g (2 oz) carrot
30ml (2 tablespoons) Heinz
    or Waistline Low-Calorie
    Salad Dressing

Shell and roughly chop the egg. Cut the carrot and cucumber
into small sticks and mix with the egg and low-calorie salad
dressing. Season to taste with salt and pepper. Take to work
packed in a carton.

Fishy Tomato Sandwich
Serves 1: 155 calories

2 slices slimmers' bread   1 small tomato
1/2 35-g (1.23-oz) pot   1 medium-sized apple *or*
    Shippam's Bloater, Crab   75g (3 oz) black grapes
    or Sardine and Tomato
    Paste

Spread both slices of bread with the fish paste and make a
sandwich with the sliced tomato. Follow your sandwich with
the fruit.

Coleslaw with Chicken
Serves 1: 160 calories

227-g (8-oz) carton Eden Vale Coleslaw in Vinaigrette
50g (2 oz) cooked chicken, no skin

Cut the chicken into small pieces and mix with the coleslaw.
Take to work in a carton.

Cottage Cheese, Crispbreads and Celery
Serves 1: 165 calories

113-g (4-oz) carton Eden Vale Cottage Cheese with
    Peppers and Onion *or* Pineapple
2 Energen crispbreads
2 sticks celery

Wash the celery sticks and take to work with the carton of
cottage cheese and crispbreads.

Spicy Chicken Sandwich with Fruit
Serves 1: 175 calories

25g (1 oz) cooked chicken, no skin
15ml (1 level tablespoon) Waistline Spicy Vegetable Spread
2 slices slimmers' bread
1 medium-sized pear *or* apple

Chop the chicken and mix with the vegetable spread. Make
into a sandwich with the two slices of bread. Follow your
sandwich with the pear or apple.

Vegetables in Blue Cheese Dressing
Serves 1: 175 calories

125g (4 oz) raw cauliflower
125g (4 oz) cucumber
30ml (2 tablespoons) Kraft
   Blue Cheese Dressing

30ml (2 tablespoons)
   natural yogurt
salt and pepper

Cut the cauliflower into florets and slice the cucumber into sticks. Mix together the blue cheese dressing and yogurt and season with salt and pepper. Stir in the vegetables. Take to work in a carton.

Soup, Yogurt and Fruit
Serves 1: 200 calories

1 sachet Batchelor's Slim-a-Soup *or* Slender Slim Soup, any flavour
1 small carton St Ivel Prize Fruit Yogurt, any flavour, *or* Eden Vale Natural Yogurt
1 medium-sized apple *or* pear

All these items could be bought on the way to work if you don't have time to prepare a packed lunch.

Make up soup as directed on packet and follow with yogurt and fruit.

Cheesy Double Decker Sandwich
Serves 1: 200 calories

15g (½ oz) Edam cheese
15ml (1 level tablespoon)
   Waistline Onion Spread
3 slices slimmers' bread

10ml (2 level teaspoons)
   low-fat spread
1 small tomato, sliced

Grate the Edam cheese and mix with the onion spread. Spread the mixture on one slice of bread. Cover with a second slice of bread and spread this with 5ml (1 level teaspoon) low-fat spread. Top with the sliced tomato. Spread the third slice of bread with the remaining low-fat spread and place on top.

Fruit and Nut Slaw
Serves 1: 200 calories

75g (3 oz) white cabbage
50g (2 oz) carrot
2 pineapple rings, canned in natural juice
1 stick celery
15g (½ oz) dry roasted peanuts

30ml (2 tablespoons) Heinz *or* Waistline Low-Calorie Salad Dressing
15ml (1 tablespoon) oil-free French dressing
salt and pepper

Shred the cabbage and grate the carrot. Cut the drained pineapple and celery into small pieces. Mix all the ingredients together and season. Pack in a food container.

Watercress and Curd Cheese Sandwich
Serves 1: 200 calories

few sprigs watercress
50g (2 oz) curd cheese *or* cottage cheese with chives

salt and pepper
2 small slices wholemeal bread, 25g (1 oz) each

Chop the watercress and mix with the curd or cottage cheese. Season with salt and pepper and use to make a sandwich with the bread.

Soup, Cottage Cheese and Crispbreads
Serves 1: 205 calories

1 sachet Batchelor's Slim-a-Soup *or* Slender Slim Soup,
  any flavour
113-g (4-oz) carton Eden Vale *or* St Ivel Cottage Cheese,
  any flavour except Onion and Cheddar
2 Energen *or* Ryvita crispbreads

All these items could be bought on the way to work if you
forget to pack up your lunch.
  Make up soup as directed on packet. Spread crispbreads
with the cottage cheese.

Barbecued Chicken Sandwich
Serves 1: 205 calories

1/2 95-g (3.35-oz) can Shippams Barbecued Chicken
  Sandwichmaker
2 small slices bread, 25g (1 oz) each
few slices cucumber

Spread the bread with the sandwichmaker and make into a
sandwich with the bread.

Rice Quick Lunch plus Fruit
Serves 1: 205 calories

1 tub KP Quick Lunch with Rice, any flavour
1 medium-sized apple, orange *or* pear

These can be bought on the way to work if you don't have
time to pack lunch.
  Make up Quick Lunch as directed on tub and follow with
the fruit.

Prawn and Tomato Chutney Roll
Serves 1: 230 calories

1 crusty bread roll
25g (1 oz) cucumber
50g (2 oz) prawns, peeled
15ml (1 level tablespoon)
    tomato chutney

5ml (1 teaspoon) oil-free
    French dressing
salt and pepper

Cut the roll in half horizontally and remove about half of the soft crumbs (these can be kept in a polythene bag in the refrigerator for up to a week and used for making bread-crumbs). Peel and dice cucumber and mix with the prawns, chutney and oil-free French dressing. Season and pile onto the roll base. Replace the top.

Fruity, Carrot and Cheese Salad
Serves 1: 230 calories

75g (3 oz) carrots
25g (1 oz) raisins *or* sultanas
1 small carton Eden Vale
    Cottage Cheese with
    Pineapple

15ml (1 tablespoon) Heinz
    or Waistline Low-Calorie
    Salad Dressing
salt and pepper

Grate the carrots and mix with raisins or sultanas, cottage cheese, salad dressing and salt and pepper. Take to work in a carton.

Chicken and Corn Relish Sandwich
Serves 1: 245 calories

50g (2 oz) cooked chicken, no skin
25g (1 oz) Bicks Corn Relish
2 small slices bread, 25g (1 oz) each

Chop the chicken and mix with the corn relish. Use to make a sandwich with the bread.

Cheese and Tomato Crispbreads
Serves 1: 245 calories

4 Energen *or* Ryvita
  crispbreads
25g (1 oz) cheese spread,
  plain *or* flavoured

1 tomato
1 medium orange *or* 75g
  (3 oz) grapes

Spread the crispbreads with the cheese and top with the
sliced tomato. Follow with fruit.

Cheese, Ham and Fruit Salad
Serves 1: 250 calories

25g (1 oz) lean cooked ham
50g (2 oz) grapes
1 stick celery
113-g (4-oz) carton Eden
  Vale Cottage Cheese with
  Pineapple

2 Energen Brancrisp *or* 2
  Ryvita Crispbreads

Chop the ham. Halve and pip the grapes and roughly chop
the celery. Mix all the ingredients together and pack in a food
container. Eat with the crispbreads. Do not spread with
butter or margarine.

Broad Bean and Ham Sausage Salad
Serves 1: 250 calories

50g (2 oz) ham sausage
175g (6 oz) broad beans,
  frozen *or* canned
30ml (2 tablespoons) Heinz
  or Waistline Low-Calorie
  Salad Dressing

15ml (1 tablespoon) tomato
  ketchup
1.25ml (¼ level teaspoon)
  mustard
salt and pepper

Cut ham sausage into small strips. Cook and drain beans. Mix together the low-calorie salad dressing, tomato ketchup, mustard and salt and pepper and then stir in the beans and ham sausage. Pack into a plastic container.

Cheese and Pineapple Salad
Serves 1: 250 calories

50g (2 oz) Edam cheese
2 pineapple rings, canned in
    natural juice
1/4 red *or* green pepper
25g (1 oz) cucumber
15ml (1 tablespoon) Heinz
    or Waistline Low-Calorie
    Salad Dressing

15ml (1 tablespoon) natural
    yogurt
salt and pepper

Cut cheese and pineapple into chunks. Discard white pith and seeds from pepper and dice flesh. Dice cucumber. Mix all the ingredients together and season with salt and pepper. Pack in a food container to take to work.

Sardine and Olive Sandwich
Serves 1: 250 calories

2 sardines in tomato sauce
1 *or* 2 stuffed olives
5ml (1 level teaspoon) onion

2 small slices bread, 25g
    (1 oz) each

Mash the sardines, chop the olives and finely chop the onion, mix the sardines, olives and onion together and sandwich between the slices of bread.

Tuna, Apple and Sweetcorn Salad
Serves 1: 250 calories

100-g (3½-oz) can tuna in
   brine
1 medium apple
lemon juice

50g (2 oz) cucumber
¼ small red *or* green pepper
45ml (3 level tablespoons)
   natural yogurt

Drain and flake the tuna. Core and dice the apple and toss
in a little lemon juice. Dice the cucumber. Discarding seeds
and pith, dice the pepper. Mix all ingredients together. Take
salad to work in a food container.

Cottage Cheese and Savoury Snacks with Fruit
Serves 1: 255 calories

113-g (4-oz) carton Eden Vale *or* St Ivel Cottage Cheese,
   any flavour except Onion and Cheddar
1 small packet Allinson's Wheateats *or* KP Wickers
1 medium-sized apple, orange *or* pear

All these items can be bought on the way to work if you forget
your packed lunch.
   Eat the cottage cheese with a packet of savoury snacks and
follow with fruit.

Chicken, Pineapple and Pepper Sandwich
Serves 1: 260 calories

50g (2 oz) cooked chicken, no skin

1 pineapple ring, canned in natural juice

15g (½ oz) red *or* green pepper

15ml (1 tablespoon) Heinz *or* Waistline Low-Calorie Salad Dressing

salt and pepper

2 small slices bread, 25g (1 oz) each

Chop chicken, pepper and drained pineapple and mix with the salad dressing. Season with salt and pepper and sandwich between the two slices of bread.

Instant Lunch and Fruit
Serves 1: 260 calories

1 KP Quick Lunch, any flavour
1 medium-sized apple *or* pear

These items can be bought on the way to work if you don't have time to pack up a lunch.

Make up Quick Lunch as directed on tub and follow with fruit.

Garlic Sausage and Baked Bean Salad
Serves 1: 265 calories

50g (2 oz) garlic sausage
¼ red *or* green pepper
1 stick celery

1 pickled onion
150-g (5.3-oz) can baked beans in tomato sauce

Cut the garlic sausage into small pieces. Discard pith and seeds from pepper and dice flesh. Roughly chop celery and slice pickled onion. Mix all the ingredients together. Pack in a container to take to work.

Salmon and Corn Salad
Serves 1: 295 calories

105-g (3.7-oz) can John
West Pink Salmon
75g (3 oz) cucumber
125g (4 oz) sweetcorn,
canned *or* cooked

30ml (2 tablespoons)
Waistline Seafood Sauce
salt and pepper

Turn the salmon into a basin and flake. Dice the cucumber.
Mix all ingredients together and season with salt and pepper.
Pack in a carton to take to work.

Danish Blue Salad
Serves 1: 295 calories

50g (2 oz) Danish Blue
Cheese
50g (2 oz) white cabbage
25g (1 oz) carrot
1 stick celery

25g (1 oz grapes)
30ml (2 tablespoons) Heinz
or Waistline Low-Calorie
Salad Dressing
salt and pepper

Cut the cheese into small cubes. Shred the cabbage, grate the
carrot and chop the celery. Halve and pip the grapes. Mix
all the ingredients together and season with salt and pepper.
Pack in a plastic container to take to work.

Cottage Cheese, Crisps and Fruit
Serves 1: 300 calories

113-g (4-oz) carton Eden Vale *or* St Ivel Cottage Cheese
with Pineapple
1 small packet Golden Wonder, KP *or* Smith's Crisps, any
flavour
1 medium-sized apple, orange *or* pear

These items can be bought on your way to work if you don't
have time to pack up a lunch.

Eat the cottage cheese with the crisps and follow with fruit.

Cheese and Pickle Crusty Roll
Serves 1: 300 calories

1 crusty roll
40g (1½ oz) Edam cheese
15ml (1 level tablespoon)
  sweet pickle

1 tomato

Cut the roll in half. Grate the Edam and mix with the sweet pickle. Use to fill the roll with the sliced tomato.

Egg Sandwich
Serves 1: 300 calories

1 egg (size 3), hardboiled
15ml (1 tablespoon) Heinz
  or Waistline Low-Calorie
  Salad Dressing
salt and pepper

mustard and cress
2 small slices bread, 25g
  (1 oz) each
1 small banana

Chop the egg and mix with the low-calorie salad dressing. Season and use to make a sandwich with a little mustard and cress and bread. Follow with the banana.

Pâté with Crispbreads and Tomato
Serves 1: 300 calories

75g (3 oz) Mattessons Ham and Tongue Pâté
4 Energen *or* Ryvita Crispbreads
2 tomatoes

Take items to work separately. Spread crispbreads with pâté and top with tomato slices.

Quick and Easy Main Meals

We have assumed that the majority of working girls will eat their main meal in the evening. But there is no reason why you shouldn't cook up one of these dishes if you happen to be at home during the middle of the day.

All the recipes are well worth cooking for one but if you would like to include the family or a friend who is also dieting, just increase the quantities accordingly. Stuffed baked potatoes make ideal and filling dieting meals. They can be baked during the evening and stored in the refrigerator ready for reheating the next day.

Some of the meals can be bought ready-made in packets or tins from shops and supermarkets and the frozen varieties can be stored in the freezer so that you always have a dieting meal available. None of the meals is difficult or takes much time to get ready. If you are the sort of person, however, who likes to nibble as soon as she gets into the kitchen, we suggest you read the section on 'Little Snacks for Nibblers'.

Calories for these main meals range from 250 to 500. If you have enough calories in your daily allowance you could choose a dessert to follow one of these meals from the selection on page 82.

Tuna and Tomato Bake
Serves 1: 250 calories

100-g (3½-oz) can John
  West Tuna in Brine
2 tomatoes
1 spring onion
25g (1 oz) fresh brown
  breadcrumbs

1.25ml (¼ level teaspoon)
  dried basil
salt and pepper
15g (½ oz) Cheddar cheese,
  grated

Drain and flake the tuna. Slice the tomatoes. Discard the
green stem of the spring onion and chop the white bulb. Mix
the spring onion with the breadcumbs and basil and season
well with salt and pepper. Spread half of the crumb mixture
over the base of a small ovenproof dish. Cover with half of
the tomato slices and then all of the tuna. Arrange the
remaining tomato on top. Add the cheese to the rest of the
crumb mixture and sprinkle over the tomatoes. Bake at
190°C (375°F), gas mark 5, for 20 minutes.

Grilled Fish and Vegetables
Serves 1: 260 calories

175g (6 oz) fillet cod *or*
  haddock
7g (¼ oz) butter *or*
  margarine

125g (4 oz) frozen mixed
  vegetables
15ml (1 tablespoon) tomato
  ketchup

Dot the fish with butter or margarine and grill. Boil the
mixed vegetables as instructed on packet, and serve with fish
and tomato ketchup.

Curried Chicken Salad
Serves 1: 260 calories

75g (3 oz) cooked chicken
45ml (3 tablespoons)
  natural yogurt
1.25ml (¼ teaspoon) lemon
  juice
1.25ml (¼ teaspoon) curry
  paste *or* powder

salt and pepper
25g (1 oz) green pepper
25g (1 oz) cucumber
1 small banana
15ml (1 level tablespoon)
  sultanas *or* raisins
lettuce

Discard any skin from the chicken and cut the flesh into
bite-size pieces. Mix together the yogurt, lemon juice and
curry paste or powder and season with salt and pepper.
Discard the white pith and seeds from the pepper and dice
the flesh. Dice the cucumber. Thickly slice the banana. Mix
the chicken with the dressing, pepper, cucumber, banana
and sultanas and serve on lettuce.

Liver, Mushrooms and Tomatoes
Serves 1: 260 calories

125g (4 oz) lamb's liver
8 squirts Limmits Spray &
  Fry
125g (4 oz) fresh
  mushrooms *or* 213-g
  (7½-oz) can mushrooms
  in brine

2 tomatoes, grilled
15ml (1 tablespoon) tomato
  ketchup *or* bottled brown
  sauce

Spray the liver with Spray & Fry and grill on both sides until
cooked. Grill the tomatoes. Poach the fresh mushrooms in
a little stock or heat the mushrooms in brine. Serve liver with
vegetables and sauce.

Minced Beef Pancakes
Serves 1: 275 calories

2 Birds Eye *or* Findus Minced Beef Pancakes
125g (4 oz) peas, frozen
15ml (1 tablespoon) tomato ketchup *or* bottled brown
   sauce

Bake or grill the pancakes as directed on packet but without added fat. Boil the peas and serve with the pancakes and ketchup or sauce.

Herby Tomato Omelette
Serves 1: 275 calories

2 tomatoes
2 eggs (size 3)
10ml (2 teaspoons) water
good pinch dried mixed
   herbs
salt and pepper

8 squirts Limmits Spray &
   Fry
1 small slice bread, 25g
   (1 oz)
7g (¼ oz) low-fat spread

Roughly chop the tomatoes. Lightly beat together the eggs, water, herbs, salt and pepper. Squirt the Spray & Fry over the surface of a small non-stick omelette pan and heat. Add the egg mixture and cook, lifting the edges and letting the soft mixture run underneath, until lightly set. Add the tomato and heat through for just a moment. Fold over and serve with bread and low-fat spread.

Chunky Soup Meal
Serves 1: 275 calories

435-g (15.3-oz) can Heinz Big Soup, Chicken & Vegetable
  or Vegetable & Lentil
1 small slice bread, 25g (1 oz)

Heat the soup and serve with the bread. Do not use butter
or margarine.

Ravioli Au Gratin
Serves 1: 280 calories

215-g (7.6-oz) can Heinz Ravioli
15g (½ oz) Cheddar cheese, grated
30ml (2 level tablespoons) fresh breadcrumbs

Heat the ravioli gently in a saucepan, then turn into a
heatproof dish. Sprinkle the cheese and breadcrumbs on top
and grill until the cheese melts and starts to brown.

Prawn Curry with Rice
Serves 1: 285 calories

1 packet Birds Eye China Dragon Prawn Curry
25g (1 oz) long-grain rice

Cook the prawn curry as instructed on the packet. Boil the
rice in salted water until soft and serve with the curry.

Fish Fingers and Peas
Serves 1: 290 calories

4 Birds Eye *or* Findus *or* Ross Fish Fingers
125g (4 oz) peas, frozen *or* canned
30ml (2 tablespoons) tomato ketchup

Grill the fish fingers without adding any fat (you will find they grill perfectly well without). Cook the peas as instructed and serve with fish fingers and tomato ketchup.

Spicy Pork and Pepper Pot
Serves 1: 290 calories

142g (5 oz) pork fillet *or* tenderloin
28g (1 oz) onion
1/4 small red *or* green pepper
113ml (4 fl. oz) bottle tomato juice cocktail
few drops Tabasco
2.5ml (1/2 teaspoon) Worcestershire sauce
salt and pepper
5ml (1 level teaspoon) cornflour
125g (4 oz) broccoli, fresh *or* frozen

Discard all visible fat from the pork and cut the lean into bite-sized pieces. Place in a small saucepan. Chop the onion. Discard the pith and seeds from the pepper and cut the flesh into strips. Add the onion and pepper to the pork with the tomato juice and Worcestershire sauce and season with salt and pepper. Cover the pan, bring to the boil and simmer very gently for 20 minutes. Blend the cornflour with a little cold water and then add to the pan, stirring all the time. Simmer for a minute. Boil the broccoli and serve with the pork.

Lamb Chop with Vegetables
Serves 1: 290 calories

125g (4 oz) broad beans, fresh, frozen *or* canned

125g (4 oz) carrots, fresh, frozen *or* canned

1 lamb chump chop, 150g (5 oz)

15ml (1 tablespoon) mint sauce

If using fresh vegetables, boil in salted water until tender (you can cook them both in the same saucepan). Cook frozen vegetables as instructed on packet or heat canned vegetables. Grill the lamb chop well and serve with vegetables and mint sauce.

Pizza with Coleslaw
Serves 1: 290 calories

5-inch Ross Cheese & Tomato *or* Ham & Mushroom Pizza
227-g (8-oz) carton Eden Vale Coleslaw in Vinaigrette

Cook the pizza as instructed on the packet and serve with the coleslaw.

Cheesy Egg and Prawns
Serves 1: 295 calories

1 egg (size 3)

125g (4 oz) broccoli, fresh *or* frozen

1/2 packet Knorr Cheese Sauce Mix

150ml (1/4 pint) skimmed milk

50g (2 oz) prawns, fresh shelled *or* frozen

50g (2 oz) sweetcorn, canned *or* cooked

Hardboil the egg, shell it and cut in half. Boil the broccoli. Make up the cheese sauce mix using skimmed milk and add the egg, prawns and sweetcorn. Heat through gently and serve with the broccoli.

Ham and Mushroom Stuffed Potato
Serves 1: 300 calories

200g (7 oz) potato
25g (1 oz) mushrooms
7g (¼ oz) low-fat spread
15ml (1 tablespoon) milk
40g (1½ oz) lean cooked
  ham

15ml (1 tablespoon) tomato
  ketchup
salt and pepper

Scrub the potato and bake it at 200°C (400°F), gas mark 6 for 1 hour, or until soft when pinched. Finely chop the mushrooms and place in a small pan with the low-fat spread and milk. Cover the pan and cook gently for a few minutes. Finely chop the ham. Cut the potato in half and scoop out the flesh leaving the shell intact. Mix with the mushrooms and their juices, ham, and tomato ketchup. Season with salt and pepper. Pile back into the potato cases and reheat at 200°C (400°F), gas mark 6, for 15 minutes.

Note You can make your stuffed potato in the evening, wrap it in clear food wrap, then store it in the refrigerator until the next day. Reheat at 200°C (400°F), gas mark 6, for 15–20 minutes.

Bacon Steak, Mushrooms and Chips
Serves 1: 300 calories

1 bacon steak, 100g (3½ oz)
125g (4 oz) grill *or* oven chips
125g (4 oz) mushrooms *or* 213-g (7½-oz) can mushrooms
  in brine

Grill bacon steak well. Grill or bake chips as instructed on packet. Poach the fresh mushrooms in a little stock, or heat canned mushrooms in brine, and serve with steak and chips.

Beef Stew and Vegetables
Serves 1: 300 calories

1 packet Birds Eye Beef Stew & Dumpling
125g (4 oz) mixed vegetables, frozen

Cook the stew as instructed on the packet. Boil the mixed vegetables and serve with the beef stew and dumplings.

Braised Kidneys with Rice
Serves 1: 305 calories

1 pack Birds Eye Braised Kidneys in Gravy
25g (1 oz) long-grain rice

Cook the kidneys as directed on the packet. Boil the rice and serve with the kidneys.

Savoury Mince
Serves 1: 305 calories

125g (4 oz) minced beef
50g (2 oz) mushrooms
30ml (2 level tablespoons) sage and onion stuffing mix
30ml (2 tablespoons) tomato ketchup
150ml (¼ pint) water
salt and pepper
125g (4 oz) cabbage, fresh *or* frozen

Brown the mince in a non-stick pan and drain off all the fat. Place the mince in a small saucepan. Chop the mushrooms and add to the saucepan with stuffing mix, tomato ketchup and water. Season well with salt and pepper. Bring to the boil, stirring continuously, and then cover the pan and simmer gently for 20 minutes. Stir occasionally and add a little more water if necessary, to prevent the mince sticking. Boil the cabbage and serve with the savoury mince.

Spicy Grilled Fish
Serves 1: 305 calories

150g (5 oz) fillet of plaice, fresh *or* frozen

5ml (1 level teaspoon) low-fat spread

25g (1 oz) Sharwood's Tomato and Chilli Chutney

25g (1 oz) Edam cheese, grated

125g (4 oz) broccoli, fresh *or* frozen

125g (4 oz) mushrooms

Dot the plaice with the low-fat spread and grill until cooked through. Spread the chutney on top and sprinkle with the grated cheese. Grill until the cheese melts. While the fish is cooking boil the broccoli and poach the mushrooms in a little salted water. Serve with the fish.

Meat Pudding with Carrots
Serves 1: 310 calories

142-g (5-oz) can Goblin's Steak and Kidney Pudding
150g (5 oz) canned carrots

Cook the steak and kidney pudding as instructed. Heat the carrots and serve with the pudding.

Casserole with Mash
Serves 1: 310 calories

1 individual Ross Beef *or* Chicken Casserole
1/2 packet Yeoman Onion *or* Bacon Savoury Mash
125g (4 oz) frozen peas

Cook the casserole as directed on the packet. Make up the mash as directed without adding butter or margarine. Boil the peas and serve with the casserole and mash.

Risotto
Serves 1: 310 calories

1 tomato
25g (1 oz) onion
50g (2 oz) long-grain rice
175ml (6 fl. oz) water
¼ beef stock cube
pinch dried basil *or* mixed
   herbs

salt and pepper
50g (2 oz) mushrooms
50g (2 oz) peas, frozen
15g (½ oz) Edam cheese,
   grated

Roughly chop the tomato and finely chop the onion. Place in a saucepan with the rice, water, stock cube, herbs and salt and pepper. Bring to the boil, stir once, cover and simmer gently for 10 minutes. Meanwhile, slice the mushrooms. Add to the pan with the peas and cook for 15 minutes longer. Add a little more water if necessary to prevent the rice sticking. Pile into a serving dish and sprinkle the cheese on top.

Kidney and Spaghetti Savoury
Serves 1: 310 calories

2 lamb's kidneys
50g (2 oz) mushrooms
1 tomato
75ml (3 fl. oz) water
¼ beef stock cube

25g (1 oz) lean cooked ham
213-g (7½-oz) can spaghetti
   in tomato sauce
salt and pepper

Halve and core the kidneys and cut into small pieces. Chop the mushrooms and tomato and place in a small saucepan with the kidneys. Bring to the boil, cover the pan and simmer gently for 10 minutes. Drain off any excess stock. Chop the ham and add to the pan with the spaghetti. Season with salt and pepper and heat through gently.

Fish and Tomato Pie
Serves 1: 315 calories

2 Findus Cod Steaks, 100g
  (3¹/₂ oz)
227-g (8-oz) can tomatoes
salt and pepper
good pinch dried basil *or*
  mixed herbs

40g (1¹/₂ oz) Edam cheese,
  grated
25g (1 oz) fresh wholemeal
  breadcrumbs
113g (4 oz) green beans,
  fresh *or* frozen

Place the frozen cod steaks in an ovenproof dish. Drain and roughly chop the tomatoes, season with salt, pepper and herbs and spoon over fish steaks. Add half of the tomato juice and discard the rest. Mix together the Edam and bread-crumbs and sprinkle on top. Cook at 190°C (375°F), gas mark 5, for 35 minutes. Brown under the grill for a few minutes. Boil the beans and serve with the fish.

Shepherd's Pie and Beans
Serves 1: 315 calories

1 Findus Shepherd's Pie, 227g (8 oz)
125g (4 oz) runner beans, frozen
15ml (1 tablespoon) tomato ketchup *or* bottled brown
  sauce

Cook the shepherd's pie as instructed on the packet. Boil the beans and serve with the pie and tomato ketchup or brown sauce.

Macaroni Cheese with Tomatoes
Serves 1: 320 calories

210-g (7.4-oz) can Heinz Macaroni Cheese
15g (½ oz) Edam Cheese
2 tomatoes

Heat the macaroni cheese as instructed on the can. Turn into
an ovenproof dish. Grate the Edam and sprinkle on top. Grill
until the cheese melts and starts to brown. Grill the tomatoes
at the same time and serve with the macaroni cheese.

Braised Liver with Vegetables
Serves 1: 320 calories

1 pack Birds Eye Liver with Onion and Gravy
½ medium packet Cadbury's Smash
125g (4 oz) baby carrots, frozen, canned *or* fresh

Cook the liver as directed on the packet. Make up the Smash
without adding butter or margarine. Boil the frozen or fresh
carrots or heat the canned carrots. Serve with the liver and
mash.

Bean and Mince Stew
Serves 1: 320 calories

125g (4 oz) minced beef
150-g (5.3-oz) can baked
  beans in tomato sauce
15ml (1 level tablespoon)
  sweet pickle
2.5ml (½ teaspoon)
  Worcestershire sauce
10ml (1 rounded teaspoon)
  dried onions
50ml (2 fl. oz) water

Brown the mince in a non-stick pan and drain off all the fat.
Place the mince in a small saucepan with all the other
ingredients and stir gently to mix. Cover the pan and simmer
gently for 15–20 minutes. Stir occasionally while

cooking and add a little more water if necessary to prevent sticking.

Note This stew can be made the night before and kept in the refrigerator ready to be reheated in a saucepan when you get home from work.

Salmon and Mushroom Supreme
Serves 1: 325 calories

1 pack Young's Salmon and Mushroom Supreme
125g (4 oz) frozen asparagus spears
125g (4 oz) frozen peas

Cook the Salmon and Mushroom Supreme as instructed on the packet. Boil the asparagus and peas and serve with the fish dish.

Pizza with Baked Tomatoes
Serves 1: 325 calories

1 Findus French Bread Pizza, Italian Style
2 tomatoes

Bake the pizza as instructed on the packet. Cut the tomatoes in half and bake alongside the pizza for the last 10 minutes.

Liver Casserole with Pasta
Serves 1: 330 calories

125g (4 oz) lamb's liver
227g (8 oz) can tomatoes
50g (2 oz) button
  mushrooms
10ml (1 rounded teaspoon)
  dried onion
15g (½ oz) pasta shapes *or*
  macaroni

good pinch mixed dried
  herbs
salt and pepper
125g (4 oz) runner beans,
  fresh *or* frozen

Slice the liver and place in a small ovenproof dish with the tomatoes and their juice. Quarter the mushrooms if large or leave whole if small. Add the mushrooms, onion, pasta and herbs to the liver and season well with salt and pepper. Cover the dish and casserole at 180°C (350°F), gas mark 4, for 35 minutes. Boil the runner beans and serve with the casserole.

Note This recipe could be prepared in the morning, put in the refrigerator, ready to pop into the oven as soon as you get home.

Stuffed Pork Chop with Vegetables
Serves 1: 335 calories

15ml (1 level tablespoon)
  sage and onion stuffing
  mix
30ml (2 tablespoons) boiling
  water
1 pork chop, 190g (6½ oz)

125g (4 oz) broccoli, fresh
  or frozen
125g (4 oz) cauliflower,
  fresh *or* frozen
15ml (1 tablespoon) apple
  sauce

Mix the stuffing mix with the boiling water and leave to stand for 15 minutes. Make a horizontal cut through the centre of the lean part of the chop to make a pocket and fill with the stuffing. Press the edges back together. Discard any large pieces of fat. Grill the chop under a moderate grill for 8–10 minutes on each side. While it is cooking boil the broccoli and cauliflower and then serve with the chop and apple sauce.

Eggy Smoked Haddock
Serves 1: 340 calories

170-g (6-oz) pack Findus Buttered Smoked Haddock
1 egg (size 3)

1 small slice bread, 25g (1 oz)
7g (¼ oz) low-fat spread

Boil the smoked haddock in the bag as instructed. Poach the egg and serve on the haddock. Spread the bread with low-fat spread and serve with egg and fish.

Lasagne with Green Beans
Serves 1: 345 calories

1 individual Birds Eye Lasagne, 250g (9 oz)
125g (4 oz) runner beans, frozen

Cook the lasagne as directed on the packet. Boil the beans and serve with the lasagne.

Cod in Shrimp Sauce with Vegetable Rice
Serves 1: 350 calories

1 Birds Eye Cod in Shrimp Flavour Sauce
½ packet Birds Eye Rice, Sweetcorn and Peppers

Cook the cod as instructed on the packet and serve with the boiled vegetable rice.

Butter Bean and Fish Soufflé
Serves 1: 360 calories

1 egg (size 2)
223-g (7.9-oz) can butter beans
35-g (1¼-oz) pot salmon and shrimp paste
5ml (1 teaspoon) lemon juice

salt and pepper
15ml (1 level tablespoon) Parmesan cheese
125g (4 oz) runner beans, frozen

Preheat the oven to 190°C (375°F), gas mark 5. Separate the egg. Place the butter beans with the liquid from the can in a liquidizer with the salmon and shrimp paste, lemon juice and egg yolk. Blend until smooth. If no liquidizer is available, rub the beans through a sieve and then mix with paste, lemon juice and egg yolk. Stir in the Parmesan cheese and season with salt and pepper. Whisk the egg white until stiff and gently fold into bean mixture. Turn into an ovenproof dish and cook in the preheated oven for 25 minutes until well risen. Boil the beans and serve with the soufflé.

Curried Mince with Rice
Serves 1: 360 calories

125g (4 oz) minced beef
3.75ml (¾ level teaspoon) curry powder
5ml (1 level teaspoon) flour
30ml (2 level tablespoons) Batchelor's Cooking Aids Mixed Vegetables

15ml (1 level tablespoon) sultanas
125ml (4 fl. oz) water
¼ beef stock cube
25g (1 oz) long-grain rice

Brown the mince in a non-stick pan and then drain off any fat. Place the mince and curry powder in a small saucepan and cook for 1 minute, stirring all the time. Stir in the flour and then add the mixed vegetables, sultanas, water and stock cube. Bring to the boil, stirring; cover the pan and simmer gently for 20 minutes. Stir occasionally and add a little more water if necessary to prevent the curry becoming too dry. While the curry is cooking, boil the rice and serve with the curry.

Chicken and Chutney Stuffed Potato
Serves 1: 365 calories

225g (8 oz) potato
50g (2 oz) cooked chicken,
  no skin
¼ small red *or* green pepper

15ml (1 tablespoon)
  skimmed milk
25g (1 oz) mango chutney
salt and pepper

Scrub the potato and bake at 200°C (400°F), gas mark 6, for 1 hour, or until soft when pinched. Chop the chicken. Discard any pith or seeds from the pepper and then dice the flesh. Cut the potato in half and scoop out the flesh leaving the shell intact. Mix the flesh with the chicken, pepper, milk and chutney. Season with salt and pepper and pile back into the potato cases. Reheat at 200°C (400°F), gas mark 6, for 15 minutes.

Note You can make your stuffed potato in the evening. Wrap it in clear food wrap, then store it in the refrigerator until next day. Reheat at 200°C (400°F), gas mark 6, for 15–20 minutes.

Sausages and Mash
Serves 1: 365 calories

2 large pork sausages
½ medium packet Cadbury's Smash
Birds *or* Boots Gravy Mix *or* Bisto Gravy Powder

Grill the pork sausages well on a rack allowing the fat to drip away. Make up Smash as instructed on the packet. Serve sausages and mash with 50ml (2 fl. oz) gravy made from any of the above mixes (do not add any fat).

Liver Parcel and Mash
Serves 1: 365 calories

1 leek
125g (4 oz) lamb's liver
1 tomato
7g (¹/₄ oz) low-fat spread
5ml (1 teaspoon) Soy sauce

pinch of mixed herbs
salt and pepper
¹/₂ medium packet
    Cadbury's Smash

Discard the tough green leaves from the leek and wash the white part thoroughly. Cut into slices and cook in boiling, salted water for 10 minutes. Drain. Cut a piece of foil large enough to completely enclose the liver and vegetables. Place the liver in the centre of the foil and cover with the leeks. Slice the tomato and place on the leeks. Dot with low-fat spread and sprinkle with Soy sauce and herbs. Season with salt and pepper and wrap up the foil to make a loose parcel. Place on a baking sheet and cook at 190°C (375°F), gas mark 5, for 20 minutes. Make up the Smash as directed and serve with the liver.

Chicken with Savoury Rice
Serves 1: 370 calories

1 chicken breast, 175g (6 oz)
¹/₂ packet Batchelor's Savoury Rice, any flavour except
    Sweet and Sour

Grill the chicken breast then remove the skin. Cook the savoury rice as instructed on the packet and serve with chicken.

Special Macaroni Cheese
Serves 1: 370 calories

50g (2 oz) macaroni
50g (2 oz) mushrooms
25g (1 oz) red *or* green
  pepper
150ml (¼ pint) skimmed
  milk

½ packet Knorr Cheese
  Sauce Mix
25g (1 oz) lean cooked ham
salt and pepper

Cook the macaroni as instructed on the packet. Slice the
mushrooms. Discard the white pith and seeds from the
pepper and dice the flesh. Blend a little of the cold milk with
the sauce mix until smooth. Place the remaining milk in a
saucepan with the pepper and mushrooms. Cover the pan
and simmer for 2–3 minutes. Strain and add the milk to the
blended sauce mix; return to the pan and bring to the boil,
stirring continuously. Simmer gently for 1 minute. Discard
any visible fat from the ham and dice the lean. Add to sauce
with the macaroni, pepper and mushrooms. Season well with
salt and pepper and reheat gently, stirring all the time.

Note The Macaroni Cheese could be made in the evening,
kept in the refrigerator, reheated gently in a saucepan,
stirring constantly, the next day.

Liver with Bacon and Beans
Serves 1: 375 calories

125g (4 oz) lamb's liver
Limmits Spray & Fry
1 rasher streaky bacon

150-g (5.3-oz) can baked
  beans in tomato sauce

Spray the liver with Spray & Fry and grill on both sides until
cooked. Grill the bacon well. Heat the baked beans and serve
with liver and bacon.

Cheese Pancakes with Beans
Serves 1: 380 calories

2 Birds Eye Cheese and Ham Pancakes *or* 2 Findus
  Cheddar Cheese Pancakes
225-g (7.9-oz) can baked beans with tomato sauce

Bake the pancakes as instructed on the packet without any
added fat. Heat the baked beans and serve with pancakes.

Chicken Espagnole with Peas
Serves 1: 385 calories

1 pack Findus Chicken Espagnole
125g (4 oz) peas, frozen

Cook the Chicken Espagnole as instructed on the packet.
Boil the peas and serve with chicken.

Sardine Stuffed Potato
Serves 1: 390 calories

200g (7 oz) potato   2 sardines in tomato sauce
113g (4 oz) cottage cheese   salt and pepper
  with chives

Scrub the potato and bake it at 200°C (400°F), gas mark 6,
for 1 hour, or until soft when pinched. Cut the potato in half
and scoop the flesh out into a basin, leaving the shell intact.
Add the cottage cheese with chives and sardines and mix well
with a fork. Season with salt and pepper and pile back into
the potato cases. Reheat at 200°C (400°F), gas mark 6, for 15
minutes.

Note You can make your stuffed potato in the evening. Wrap
it in clear food wrap, then store it in the refrigerator until the
next day. Reheat at 200°C (400°F), gas mark 6, for 15–20
minutes.

Tuna and Sweetcorn Stuffed Potato
Serves 1: 390 calories

200g (7 oz) potato
100-g (3½-oz) can tuna in
  brine
50g (2 oz) curd *or* cottage
  cheese

25g (1 oz) sweetcorn
salt and pepper

Scrub the potato and bake it at 200°C (400°F), gas mark 6, for 1 hour, or until soft when pinched. Cut the potato in half lengthwise leaving the shell intact and scoop the flesh out into a basin. Drain the tuna and add to the potato with the curd or cottage cheese and sweetcorn. Season with salt and pepper and pile back into the potato cases. Reheat at 200°C (400°F), gas mark 6, for 15 minutes.

Note You can make your stuffed potato in the evening. Wrap it in clear food wrap, then store it in the refrigerator until the next day. Reheat at 200°C (400°F), gas mark 6, for 15–20 minutes.

Chicken with Sweetcorn and Potato Croquettes
Serves 1: 390 calories

1 chicken breast, 175g (6 oz)
125g (4 oz) sweetcorn, canned *or* frozen
3 Birds Eye, Findus *or* Ross potato croquettes

Grill the chicken breast until tender. Cook sweetcorn as instructed on packet or can. Bake the potato croquettes without adding fat until cooked through and slightly browned.

Sausages, Bacon and Beans
Serves 1: 390 calories

2 pork chipolatas
2 rashers streaky bacon
225-g (7.9-oz) can baked beans in tomato sauce

Grill the chipolatas and bacon well on a rack allowing fat to drip away. Serve with heated baked beans in tomato sauce.

Bean, Egg and Potato Grill
Serves 1: 390 calories

1 rasher streaky bacon
1/2 medium packet
  Cadbury's Smash
1 egg (size 3)

150-g (5.3-oz) can baked
  beans in tomato sauce
15g (1/2 oz) grated Edam
  cheese

Crisply grill the bacon and cut into small pieces. Make up the Smash as directed on the packet and then stir in the bacon. Spread this mixture over the base of an ovenproof dish and keep warm. Poach the egg and heat the baked beans. Place the egg on the potato, cover with the beans and sprinkle the cheese on top. Grill until the cheese melts and serve immediately.

Chicken and Cauliflower Curry
Serves 1: 340 calories

75g (3 oz) cooked chicken,
  no skin
75g (3 oz) cauliflower, fresh
  or frozen
1/2 packet Colman's Curry
  Mix, any flavour

150ml (1/4 pint) water
15ml (1 level tablespoon)
  sultanas
25g (1 oz) long-grain rice

Cut the chicken into bite-sized pieces. If fresh cauliflower is used cut it into florets. Boil the cauliflower until just tender. Blend the curry mix with water and bring to the boil, stirring continuously. Add the chicken, cauliflower and sultanas; cover the pan and simmer for 10 minutes. Stir occasionally and add a little extra water if necessary to prevent the sauce sticking. Meanwhile boil the rice and serve with the curry.

Note The curry could be made in the evening, kept in the refrigerator, and reheated gently in a saucepan, stirring frequently, the next day.

Beef Curry, Rice and Cucumber Salad
Serves 1: 400 calories

1 Birds Eye Beef Curry with Rice	little chopped mint *or* pinch dried mint
75g (3 oz) cucumber	salt and pepper
15ml (1 tablespoon) natural low-fat yogurt	

Cook the curry as instructed on packet. Dice the cucumber and mix with yogurt and mint. Season with salt and pepper and serve as a side salad with the curry.

Roast Chicken Dinner
Serves 1: 400 calories

150g (5 oz) new potatoes *or* 175g (6 oz) canned new potatoes, drained	150g (5 oz) canned carrots, drained
1 packet Birds Eye Gravy and Roast Chicken	30ml (2 level tablespoons) stuffing made with packet mix

Scrub and boil the new potatoes if raw; heat if canned. Heat the roast chicken in gravy and carrots. Serve with stuffing.

Soup, Beefburgers and Beans
Serves 1: 400 calories

1 Boots, Heinz *or* Waistline low-calorie soup, any flavour
2 Findus beefburgers
225-g (7.9-oz) can baked beans in tomato sauce

Heat the soup as instructed and serve as a starter. Grill the
beefburgers well on a rack, letting any fat drip away. Heat
the baked beans and serve with beefburgers.

French Bread Pizza with Coleslaw
Serves 1: 405 calories

1 Findus French Bread Pizza, any flavour except Barbecue
   Beef
227-g (8-oz) carton Eden Vale Salad in Vinaigrette

Cook the pizza as directed on the packet and serve with the
coleslaw.

Fruity Baconburgers with Vegetables
Serves 1: 415 calories

2 Birds Eye Baconburgers
2 rings pineapple canned in
   natural juice, drained
little mustard
15g (½ oz) Edam cheese
125g (4 oz) Birds Eye Stir
   Fry Continental
   Vegetables

Grill the baconburgers on a rack letting the fat drip away.
Spread with the mustard and place the pineapple rings on
top. Sprinkle on the cheese and grill for a few minutes more
until the cheese melts. Cook the vegetables as instructed and
serve with the baconburgers.

Beef Risotto
Serves 1: 420 calories

1 individual packet Vesta Beef Risotto

Cook the risotto as instructed. The calories include the fat you were told to add.

Mixed Grill with Spaghetti
Serves 1: 420 calories

2 lamb's kidneys
a little oil
2 rashers streaky bacon

1 pork chipolata
213-g (7½-oz) can spaghetti
 in tomato sauce

Brush the kidneys with a little oil and grill. Grill the bacon and chipolata well. Heat the spaghetti in tomato sauce and serve with mixed grill.

Moussaka with Tomato Salad
Serves 1: 440 calories

1 Findus Moussaka, 397g
 (14 oz)
2 tomatoes
1 spring onion *or*
 5ml (1 level teaspoon)
 chopped raw onion

15ml (1 tablespoon) oil-free
 French dressing

Cook the Moussaka as instructed on the packet. Slice the tomatoes. Finely chop the spring onion or onion and sprinkle over the tomatoes. Spoon over the oil-free French dressing and serve with the Moussaka.

Plaice and Chips
Serves 1: 445 calories

150g (5 oz) fillet plaice
7g (¼ oz) butter
125g (4 oz) grill *or* oven
  chips
15ml (1 tablespoon)
  Waistline Tartare Sauce

or 15 ml (1 tablespoon)
tomato ketchup
125g (4 oz) frozen *or* canned
  garden peas

Dot the plaice with butter and grill. Grill or bake oven chips as instructed on packet. Boil peas and drain. Serve with fish and tartare sauce or ketchup.

Toad in the Hole with Beans
Serves 1: 465 calories

1 Findus Toad-in-the-Hole, 170g (6 oz)
150-g (5.3-oz) can baked beans with tomato sauce

Cook the toad in the hole as directed on the packet. Heat the baked beans and serve with toad-in-the-hole.

Cheese Flan with Tomatoes
Serves 1: 490 calories

1 small Birds Eye Cheese, Egg and Onion Flan, 142g
  (5 oz)
2 tomatoes
15ml (1 tablespoon) bottled brown sauce

Cook the flan as instructed on the packet. Cut the tomatoes in half and bake next to the flan for the last 10 minutes. Serve with brown sauce.

Crispy Cod with Mushy Peas
Serves 1: 490 calories

2 Birds Eye Oven Crispy   ½ 304-g (10.7-oz) can
  Cod Steaks   Batchelor's Mushy Peas
vinegar (optional)
15ml (1 tablespoon) tomato
  ketchup

Bake the cod steaks as instructed on packet, then drain away
any fat. Sprinkle with a little vinegar if liked. Heat the mushy
peas gently in a small saucepan and serve with the fish and
tomato ketchup.

Steak and Chips
Serves 1: 495 calories

1 rump steak, 175g (6 oz)   1 tomato
5ml (1 teaspoon) mustard   125g (4 oz) grill *or* oven
50g (2 oz) mushrooms   chips

Medium or well grill the rump steak, cutting off any large
chunks of fat. Poach the mushrooms in a little stock and grill
the tomato. Grill or bake the chips as instructed on packet
and serve with steak and vegetables.

Low-calorie Diet Savers

These simple-to-prepare snack meals are ideal diet-savers when you have used up most of your calorie allowance during the day and have little left for your evening meal. For example, there may be the occasion when you lunch out on business or with friends, and aren't sure how much damage you've done to your diet. If a rather lavish lunch is balanced with a low-calorie breakfast and one of these diet savers, you shouldn't actually put on any pounds.

Some people prefer to have several small meals during the day than to have two or three large meals. And this little-and-often pattern of eating has a slight dieting advantage in speeding up your metabolic rate for more periods during the day. If you choose any of the meals in this section you could have as many as five during a day and still keep to a fast-slimming 1000 calories. For other low-calorie snack meals see the sections on Breakfasts and Packed Lunches.

It's probably a good idea to keep some diet-saving items, such as snack pizzas or frozen cod in sauce, in your freezer so that if disaster strikes you have no excuse to give up dieting. You will feel happier if you always try to foresee when problems are likely to crop up and make sure you plan for low-calorie meals during the rest of the day. That way you know you are coping as best you can and have no feelings of being a failure. Nobody is perfect and there are bound to be days when it is difficult to diet, but everyone can lose weight if really determined to succeed.

Savoury Grilled Toast
Serves 1: 135 calories

1 small slice bread, 25g (1 oz)
1 tomato
1 Birds Eye Griller, Mushroom and Bacon *or* Pizza

Toast the bread. Slice the tomato and place on top. Cover with the Griller and grill until melted.

Toasted Sandwich
Serves 1: 145 calories

1 Findus Toasted Sandwich, Ham & Cheese

Grill the toasted sandwich without any added fat and serve.

Creamed Mushrooms on Toast
Serves 1: 145 calories

¼ chicken stock cube
125ml (4 fl. oz) water
125g (4 oz) button
    mushrooms
30ml (2 level tablespoons)
    powdered skimmed milk
10ml (2 level teaspoons)
    cornflour
salt and pepper
1 small slice bread, 25g
    (1 oz)

Crumble the stock cube in 75ml (3 fl. oz) water and use to poach mushrooms in a covered pan for 5 minutes. Blend the powdered skimmed milk and cornflour with the remaining water and add to the pan. Bring to the boil, stirring continuously, and cook for 1 minute. Season with salt and pepper. Toast the bread and serve the mushrooms on top.

Fish in Butter Sauce
Serves 1: 165 calories

1 packet Ross Cod *or* Haddock in Butter Sauce
125g (4 oz) runner beans, frozen

Cook the fish in sauce as directed on packet. Boil the beans
and serve with the fish.

Eggy Tomato Toast
Serves 1: 165 calories

1 tomato
1 egg (size 2)
salt and pepper

pinch of mixed herbs
1 small slice bread, 25g
(1 oz)

Skin the tomato. Cut in half and squeeze out the seeds and
juice. Chop the flesh and place in a non-stick pan. Lightly
beat the egg and season with salt, pepper and herbs. Add to
the tomato and stir over a low heat until creamy. Toast the
bread and serve the egg mixture on top.

Crab and Asparagus Toast
Serves 1: 170 calories

1 small slice bread, 25g
(1 oz)
½ 42-g (1½-oz) can dressed
crab
3 asparagus spears, canned
or cooked

1 Kraft Cheddar *or*
Cheshire Singles Cheese
Slice

Toast the bread and spread with the crab. Arrange the
drained asparagus spears on top and cover with the cheese.
Grill until the cheese melts and the asparagus is hot.

Cod in Parsley Sauce
Serves 1: 175 calories

1 packet Findus Cod in Parsley Sauce, 170g (6 oz)
125g (4 oz) mixed vegetables, frozen

Cook the cod in sauce as directed on the packet. Boil the
mixed vegetables and serve with the fish.

Baked Beans on Toast
Serves 1: 175 calories

1 small slice bread, 28g (1 oz)
150-g (5.3-oz) can baked beans with tomato sauce

Toast the bread. Heat the beans and serve on the toast.

Tasty Blue Cheese Toast
Serves 1: 180 calories

25g (1 oz) Danish blue   onion salt
  cheese   black pepper
10ml (2 level teaspoons)   1 small slice bread, 25g
  tomato chutney   (1 oz)
few drops Worcestershire
  sauce

Mix together the Danish blue cheese, tomato chutney and
Worcestershire sauce. Season with a little onion salt and
black pepper. Toast the bread on one side only. Spread the
untoasted side with the cheese mixture and grill until
melted.

Banana and Bacon Toast
Serves 1: 180 calories

1 rasher streaky bacon
1 small banana
1 small slice bread, 25g (1 oz)

Grill the bacon rasher until crisp and break into small pieces.
Peel and mash the banana. Toast the bread and spread the
banana on top. Heat under the grill and sprinkle with the
bacon pieces.

Prawn Salad
Serves 1: 190 calories

1 tomato	onions
lettuce	carrots
cucumber	125g (4 oz) peeled prawns
cress	30ml (2 tablespoons)
peppers	Waistline Seafood Sauce
radishes	

Make a mixed salad from any of the above vegetables in as
large a quantity as you wish. Serve with prawns and seafood
sauce.

Ham, Pineapple and Cheese Toast
Serves 1: 200 calories

1 small slice bread, 25g (1 oz)	1 ring pineapple, canned in natural juice
mustard	1 Kraft Cheddar *or*
25g (1 oz) slice lean cooked ham	Cheshire Singles Cheese Slice

Toast the bread and then spread thinly with a little mustard.
Discard any visible fat from the ham and lay the slice on the
toast. Top with the pineapple ring and then the cheese. Grill
until the cheese is melted and the topping is hot.

Chicken and Sweetcorn Toast
Serves 1: 200 calories

25g (1 oz) cooked chicken
25g (1 oz) sweetcorn,
  canned *or* cooked
15ml (1 tablespoon)
  low-calorie salad cream

15g (½ oz) Edam cheese
salt and pepper
1 small slice bread, 25g
  (1 oz)

Discard any skin from the chicken, and chop the flesh. Mix with the sweetcorn, low-calorie salad cream and grated Edam cheese. Season with salt and pepper. Toast the bread on one side only. Spread the chicken mixture on the untoasted side and grill until hot.

Chicken Casserole with Vegetables
Serves 1: 200 calories

1 packet Birds Eye Chicken and Mushroom Casserole
125g (4 oz) Birds Eye Peas and Baby Carrots

Cook the casserole as instructed on the packet. Boil the peas and baby carrots and serve with the casserole.

Fish Cakes with Vegetables
Serves 1: 205 calories

2 fish cakes
1 tomato
125g (4 oz) peas, frozen *or*
  canned

15ml (1 tablespoon) tomato
  ketchup

Grill the fish cakes without added fat until cooked through. Grill the tomato. Boil the peas and serve with fish cakes, tomato and tomato ketchup.

Cauliflower Cheese
Serves 1: 205 calories

225g (8 oz) cauliflower,
   fresh *or* frozen
½ packet Knorr Cheese
   Sauce Mix
150ml (¼ pint) skimmed
   milk

15g (½ oz) Cheddar cheese
15ml (1 level tablespoon)
   fresh breadcrumbs

If the cauliflower is fresh, trim off any leaves and the hard
stalk. Cook in boiling, salted water until just tender and then
drain. If the cauliflower is frozen, cook as instructed on the
packet and drain. Place the cauliflower in a heatproof dish
and keep warm. Make up the sauce mix with the skimmed
milk and pour over the cauliflower. Sprinkle the cheese and
breadcrumbs on top and cook under a moderate grill until
the cheese melts and starts to brown.

Savoury Pancakes with Grilled Tomatoes
Serves 1: 215 calories

2 Birds Eye Savoury Pancakes, Pizza flavour
2 tomatoes

Grill or bake the pancakes without added fat. Grill the
tomatoes and serve with the pancakes.

Pizza with Tomato Salad
Serves 1: 220 calories

1 Findus Crusty Bun Pizza
2 tomatoes
little chopped onion *or*
   chives

15ml (1 tablespoon) oil-free
   French dressing

Cook the pizza as instructed. Slice the tomatoes and sprinkle
with the onion or chives and French dressing.

Chicken, Pasta Shells and Beans
Serves 1: 225 calories

1 Findus Devon Platter

Cook the Devon Platter as instructed on the packet.

Cheesy Egg on Toast
Serves 1: 225 calories

1 egg (size 2)	salt and pepper
50g (2 oz) St Ivel Cottage Cheese with Onion and Cheddar	1 small slice bread, 25g (1 oz)

Lightly beat the egg and mix with the cottage cheese. Season with salt and pepper and cook in a non-stick pan over a low heat, stirring continuously, until creamy. Toast the bread and serve the cheesy egg on toast.

Ravioli
Serves 1: 230 calories

215-g (7.6-oz) can Heinz Ravioli
15ml (1 level tablespoon) Parmesan cheese, grated

Heat the ravioli in a small pan over a low heat. Turn into a bowl and sprinkle the Parmesan on top.

Smoked Haddock with Peas
Serves 1: 230 calories

170g (6 oz) Findus Smoked Haddock
125g (4 oz) peas, frozen

Boil the smoked haddock in the bag as instructed and add the peas to the pan for the last 4 minutes. Serve the peas with the haddock.

Cod in Cheese or Mushroom Sauce
Serves 1: 235 calories

1 packet Birds Eye Cod in Cheese *or* Mushroom Sauce, 170g (6 oz)
125g (4 oz) Birds Eye Peas and Baby Carrots

Cook the cod in cheese or mushroom sauce as instructed on the packet. Boil the peas and baby carrots in the same pan for the last 4 minutes. Serve the vegetables with the fish.

Pork and Coleslaw Salad
Serves 1: 240 calories

75g (3 oz) lean roast pork
50g (2 oz) white cabbage
25g (1 oz) carrot
25g (1 oz) green *or* red pepper
1 spring onion

30ml (2 tablespoons) Heinz *or* Waistline Low-Calorie Salad Dressing
1.25ml (1/4 level teaspoon) mustard
salt and pepper

Discard any visible fat from the pork. Shred the cabbage, grate the carrot and chop the pepper and spring onion. Mix the low-calorie salad dressing with the mustard and season with salt and pepper. Mix the vegetables with the dressing and serve with pork.

Minced Beef with Mashed Potato
Serves 1: 245 calories

1 individual Ross Minced Beef and Vegetables
½ medium packet Cadbury's Smash

Cook the minced beef as instructed on the packet. Make up the potato as instructed and serve with the meat.

Ham Sausage with Coleslaw
Serves 1: 245 calories

113g (4 oz) pack Mattesson's Ham Sausage
227-g (8-oz) carton Eden Vale Vinaigrette Salad *or* 142-g
   (5-oz) carton St Ivel Coleslaw in Low-Calorie Dressing

Serve the ham sausage with one of the above cartons of coleslaw.

Soup with Bread
Serves 1: 250 calories

425-g (15-oz) can Campbells Main Course Vegetable Soup
1 small slice bread, 25g (1 oz)

Heat the soup and serve with the bread (do not add butter or margarine).

Cottage Cheese with Salad
Serves 1: 250 calories

1 tomato
lettuce
cucumber
cress
pepper
radishes
onions
carrots
170-g (6-oz) carton Eden
  Vale Cottage Cheese with
  Salmon & Cucumber *or*
  170-g (6-oz) carton St
  Ivel Cottage Cheese with
  Vegetables and Ham

15ml (1 tablespoon) Heinz
  or Waistline Low-Calorie
  Salad Dressing

Make a mixed salad from any of the above salad vegetables
in as large as quantity as you wish. Serve with cottage cheese
of your choice and salad dressing.

Roast Beef and Mash
Serves 1: 255 calories

1 packet Birds Eye Gravy
  and Lean Roast Beef,
  113g (4 oz)
125g (4 oz) Brussels
  sprouts, fresh *or* frozen
125g (4 oz) baby carrots,
  fresh, frozen *or* canned

½ medium packet
  Cadbury's Smash
5ml (1 level teaspoon)
  horseradish sauce

Cook the Gravy and Lean Roast Beef as instructed on the
packet. Boil the Brussels sprouts and carrots. Make up the
Smash as instructed. Serve all the vegetables with the beef
and horseradish sauce.

Desserts and Sweet Treats

If you have a sweet tooth your best plan is to include a low-calorie dessert or sweet treat in your day's menu so you don't feel deprived. That way there is less likelihood of your bingeing on high-calorie sweet temptations. Here we have selected some dessert recipes that are well worth making just for one – but if you want to serve them to your family and friends, you can just increase the ingredients accordingly.

If you don't have time to make your own dessert, there are many ready-made individual puddings and yogurts available in supermarkets and shops. Don't be tempted, though, to buy more than one dessert a day. You may intend to eat just one but the chances are that you'll end up eating the lot if it is sitting calling at you from the refrigerator.

Ice cream is an excellent dessert for slimmers. Again we suggest you buy ice cream in individual bars or tubs. Not only is it difficult to accurately measure a portion if it is scooped from a family-size pack, but the temptation will be there to go back for another scoop . . . and another scoop.

Fresh fruit is the lowest calorie dessert that you can eat and you will find a calorie list in our basic foods section on page 138. There are also a number of fruits canned in natural juice or low-calorie syrup now available and we have included a list in this chapter. Don't assume, though, that fruit in sugar syrup will cost little more. A 425-g (15-oz) can of apricot halves in syrup could cost as much as 450 calories compared with 70 calories for the same amount in low-calorie syrup.

Spiced Poached Pear
Serves 1: 70 calories

1 firm pear
4 cloves
75ml (3 fl. oz) apple juice

Peel, core and quarter the pear. Stud each quarter with a clove. Place in a small saucepan with the apple juice and simmer gently until the pear is tender. The time this takes will depend on how firm the pear is, but it should be at least 15 minutes. Remove the cloves and serve pear warm or cold.

Honey-poached Pear
Serves 1: 90 calories

1 firm pear
75ml (3 fl. oz) apple juice
5ml (1 level teaspoon) honey

Peel, quarter and core the pear and place in a small saucepan with the apple juice and honey. Cover the pan and simmer gently until the pear is tender. The time this takes will depend on how firm the pear is, but it should be at least 15 minutes. Occasionally turn the pear in the juice while poaching. Serve pear with honey sauce warm or cold.

Baked Banana with Rum
Serves 1: 100 calories

1 small banana
15ml (1 tablespoon) pineapple juice
5ml (1 level teaspoon) caster sugar
5ml (1 teaspoon) rum

Peel the banana and place on a piece of foil large enough to completely enclose it. Sprinkle on the pineapple juice, caster sugar and rum and wrap up to make a loose parcel. Place on a baking sheet and cook for 15 minutes at 190°C (375°F), gas mark 5. Serve hot.

Blackberry Baked Apple
Serves 1: 115 calories

1 cooking apple, 225g (8 oz)
50g (2 oz) fresh *or* frozen blackberries
5ml (1 level teaspoon) honey

Core the apple and make a cut through the skin around the middle. Stand in a small ovenproof dish and fill the apple cavity with blackberries and honey. Pour enough water into the dish to come ¼-inch up the sides of the apple. Bake the apple at 190°C (375°F), gas mark 5, for 25–35 minutes or until soft.

Apricot Mousse
Serves 1: 140 calories

50g (2 oz) dried apricots
75ml (3 fl. oz) water
strip of lemon rind
5ml (1 teaspoon) lemon
  juice
5ml (1 level teaspoon)
  honey
1 egg white (size 3)

Soak dried apricots in the water overnight, then put into a small saucepan with lemon rind, lemon juice and honey. Cover and simmer gently until really tender – about 20 minutes. Discard the lemon rind and either rub the apricots and juice through a sieve, or purée in a blender. Leave until cold. Whisk the egg white until stiff but not dry and fold into the apricot purée. Turn into a bowl or glass and chill.

Peach Melba
Serves 1: 145 calories

50g (2 oz) fresh *or* frozen
   raspberries
5ml (1 level teaspoon) sugar
220-g (7.8-oz) can Boots
   Peaches in Low-Calorie
   Syrup

1 Lyons Maid Vanilla Ice
   Cream Bar

Crush the raspberries with the sugar. Drain the peaches and
discard the syrup. Place the peaches in the base of a sundae
glass with the ice cream on top. Pour the raspberry sauce over
and serve immediately.

Baked Apple with Mincemeat
Serves 1: 145 calories

1 cooking apple, 225g (8 oz)
25g (1 oz) mincemeat

Core the apple and make a cut through the skin around the
middle. Place in an ovenproof dish. Fill the apple cavity with
mincemeat. Pour in enough water to come ¼ inch up the side
of the apple and bake at 190°C (375°F), gas mark 5, for 25–35
minutes until soft.

Baked Apple with Sultanas
Serves 1: 145 calories

1 cooking apple, 225g (8 oz)
30ml (2 level tablespoons) sultanas
5ml (1 level teaspoon) sugar

Core the apple and make a cut through the skin around the
middle. Place apple in a small ovenproof dish and fill centre
with sultanas and sugar. Pour in enough water to come ¼

inch up the side of the apple and bake at 190°C (375°F), gas mark 5, for 25–35 minutes until soft.

Pear, Walnut and Yogurt Dessert
Serves 1: 170 calories

1 medium pear
2 walnut halves
1 small carton natural yogurt

Quarter, core and dice the pear. There is no need to peel it. Roughly chop the walnuts and mix with the yogurt and pear. Serve immediately.

Baked Egg Custard
Serves 1: 175 calories

1 egg (size 3)
10ml (2 level teaspoons)
  sugar

125ml (4 fl. oz)
  semi-skimmed milk
pinch grated nutmeg

Lightly beat the egg and sugar in a basin until just blended. Heat the milk until hot but not boiling and then pour onto the eggs and sugar, whisking all the time. Strain into a small ovenproof dish and sprinkle the nutmeg on top. Stand the dish in a roasting tin containing ½-inch boiling water and bake at 170°C (325°F), gas mark 3, for 30–35 minutes or until set. Serve warm or cold.

Fresh Fruit Jelly
Serves 1: 185 calories

¹/₄ packet jelly cubes, any flavour
50g (2 oz) grapes
1 small banana

Dissolve the jelly in 50ml (2 fl. oz) boiling water in a measuring jug. Make up to 150ml (¹/₄ pint) with ice cubes. Stir until the ice cubes melt and pour the jelly into a dish. Halve and pip the grapes. Peel and slice the banana. Add the fruit to the jelly and chill until set.

Note If you do not have any ice cubes use cold water but chill the jelly well before adding the fruit. The remaining jelly cubes will keep well in the cupboard providing that they are wrapped in clear food wrap. This recipe can be made the evening before and kept in the refrigerator.

Chocolate Creamed Rice
Serves 1: 190 calories

| 150ml (¹/₄ pint) semi-skimmed milk | 5ml (1 level teaspoon) sugar |
| 15ml (1 level tablespoon) drinking chocolate powder | 30ml (2 level tablespoons) pudding *or* round-grained rice |

Heat the milk and then stir in the drinking chocolate and sugar. Pour into a basin and add the rice. Cover with foil and stand the basin over a pan of simmering water. Cook for ³/₄–1 hour or until creamy. Stir occasionally while cooking. Remove cover for last 15 minutes. Serve hot or leave until cold.

Banana and Custard
Serves 1: 190 calories

15ml (1 level tablespoon) custard powder
10ml (2 level teaspoons) sugar
125ml (4 fl. oz) semi-skimmed milk
1 small banana

Blend the custard powder with the sugar and a little semi-skimmed milk until smooth. Heat the remaining milk to boiling point and then pour onto the custard powder mixture, stirring. Return to the pan and bring to the boil, stirring continuously. Simmer for a minute. Peel the banana and slice into a bowl. Pour on the custard and serve.

Rice Pudding with Sultanas
Serves 1: 190 calories

30ml (2 level tablespoons) pudding *or* round-grain rice
150ml (¼ pint) semi-skimmed milk
15ml (1 level tablespoon) sultanas
5ml (1 level teaspoon) honey

Place all the ingredients in a basin and stand it over a saucepan of simmering water. Cover with a piece of foil. Alternatively, you could use a double boiler. Cook for ¾–1 hour or until creamy, stirring occasionally. Remove cover for last 15 minutes. Serve hot.

Pears Belle Hélène
Serves 1: 195 calories

220-g (7.8-oz) can Boots Pears in Low-Calorie Syrup
1 Walls Cornish Ice Cream Bar *or* Golden Vanilla Ice Cream Bar
15ml (1 level tablespoon) Chocolate Dessert Sauce
5ml (1 level teaspoon) chopped nuts

Drain the pears and arrange in a sundae glass. Place the ice cream on top and then pour over the sauce. Sprinkle with nuts and serve immediately.

Baked Apricot Custard
Serves 1: 200 calories

4 dried apricot halves
1 egg (size 3)
5ml (1 level teaspoon)
   honey

125ml (4 fl. oz)
   semi-skimmed milk
pinch grated nutmeg

Soak the apricots in water for several hours or overnight. Drain and pat dry with kitchen paper. Place in a small ovenproof dish. Lightly whisk together the egg and honey until just blended. Heat the milk until hot but not boiling and then pour onto the egg, whisking continuously. Strain over the apricots and sprinkle the nutmeg on top. Stand the dish in a roasting tin containing 1/2-inch boiling water and bake at 170°C (325°F), gas mark 3, for 30–35 minutes or until set. Serve warm or cold.

Choc Bar with Tangy Orange Sauce
Serves 1: 205 calories

15ml (1 tablespoon)
   unsweetened orange juice
15ml (1 level tablespoon)
   orange marmalade

1 Walls Dark and Golden *or*
   Golden Vanilla Choc Bar
5ml (1 level teaspoon)
   chocolate vermicelli

Heat the orange juice and marmalade together in a small saucepan until the marmalade has melted. Simmer for a minute watching carefully to make sure it doesn't burn. Place the ice cream in a sundae glass and pour the hot sauce on top. Sprinkle on the chocolate vermicelli and serve immediately.

Apple, Muesli and Yogurt Dessert
Serves 1: 210 calories

1 medium apple
30ml (2 level tablespoons) muesli
1 small carton natural yogurt

Quarter, core and dice the apple. There is no need to peel
it. Mix with the muesli and yogurt and serve immediately.

Banana, Nut and Yogurt Dessert
Serves 1: 220 calories

15g (½ oz) toasted hazelnuts
1 small banana
1 small carton natural yogurt

Roughly chop the hazelnuts. Peel and slice the banana and
mix with yogurt and nuts. Serve immediately.

Yogurts

	Calories
St Michael Natural	105
Eden Vale Natural	110
Dessert Farm Peach and Redcurrant *or* Pear and Banana	110
St Ivel Prize Fruit	110
Dessert Farm Strawberry	115
Raines Mr Men's	115
Dessert Farm Blackcurrant	120
St Ivel Country Prize Grapefruit Muesli	120
Chambourcy Melon and Orange	125
Dessert Farm Mandarin and Grapefruit *or* Raspberry	125
St Michael Pineapple	125
St Ivel Country Prize Walnut Muesli	125

St Ivel Hazelnut	125
Chambourcy Black Cherry, Rhubarb, Peach and Redcurrant *or* Strawberry	130
Dessert Farm Black Cherry *or* Strawberry Surprise	130
Eden Vale Natural with Grapefruit	130
Raines Fruit	130
St Michael Jaffa Orange	130
Chambourcy Pear and Banana	135
Dessert Farm Raspberry Surprise	135
Waitrose, all flavours	135
St Ivel Country Prize Muesli	135
Raines Hazelnut	140
Ski, all flavours	140
St Michael Strawberry	140
Eden Vale Banana, Lemon and Lime *or* Vanilla	145
Eden Vale Natural with Honey	145
Sainsbury's Banana	145
St Michael Black Cherry	145
Eden Vale Tropical, Apricot and Mango	145
Chambourcy Lemon Curd	150
Raines Muesli	150
Sainsbury's Hazelnut	150
St Ivel Countess, all flavours	150
St Michael Peach Melba *or* Raspberry	150
Eden Vale Tropical, Passion Fruit and Melon *or* Pineapple and Coconut	150
Eden Vale Chocolate	160
St Michael Apricot and Almond	160
Eden Vale Tropical, Melon and Ginger	160
St Michael Muesli	170
Sainsbury's Black Cherry	175
Sainsbury's Chocolate	180

PUDDINGS

per individual carton unless otherwise stated	Calories
Boots Low-Calorie Dessert Mix, Banana, Butterscotch, Peach *or* Strawberry, per serving made up	65
Findus Lemon Yoghurt Mouse	75
Carnation Slim Sweet, per sachet made up	80
Findus Black Cherry Yoghurt Mouse	80
Findus Strawberry Vanilla Double Mousse	80
Chambourcy Flanby Caramel	90
Ross Mousse Cups, all flavours	100
Findus Chocolate Mousse	105
Findus Strawberry Ripple	105
Findus Raspberry Ripple	105
Birds Eye Mousse, all flavours	110
Chambourcy Tropical Fruit Sundae	110
Birds Eye Super Mousse	120
Chambourcy Cocktail Fruit Sundae	120
Chambourcy Strawberry Dalky	120
Ross Crème Caramel	120
Chambourcy Chocolate and Vanilla Supreme Dessert	125
Chambourcy Raspberry Fruit Sundae	125
Chambourcy Strawberry Sundae Special	125
Birds Eye Melba, all flavours	130
Birds Eye Trifle, all flavours	130
Chambourcy Chocolate Dalky	130
Chambourcy Mint and Chocolate Supreme Dessert	140
St Michael Raspberry Royale	140
Chambourcy Chocolate Chamby	145
Sainsbury's Chilled Mousse	145
Chambourcy Strawberry and Vanilla Supreme Dessert	150
St Michael Mandarin Royale	150
Eden Vale Chocolate Fresh Cream Dessert	160
Ross Devonshire Trifle, all flavours	160

Ambrosia Creamed Rice, snack-size can	165
Eden Vale Raspberry Fool	165
St Ivel Fruit Wizard Mousse	165
St Ivel Trifle, all flavours	165
Eden Vale Strawberry Fool	175
St Michael Caramel Desert	175
St Michael Caramel *or* Chocolate Delight	180
Eden Vale Syllabub	185
St Michael Chocolate Dessert	185
St Ivel Fruit Cream Dessert	190
St Ivel Chocolate Fresh Cream Dessert	195
Birds Eye Star Turn	200
St Ivel Soufflé, Fruit	205
Birds Eye Lovely	220
Eden Vale Black Cherry *or* Strawberry Cheesecake	225
St Ivel Cheesecake, Strawberry *or* Blackcurrant	225
Chambourcy Blackcurrant Cheesecake	230
St Ivel Soufflé, Chocolate	235

Ice Cream

	Calories
Lyons Maid Vanilla Bar	70
Lyons Maid Gold Seal Raspberry Sundae	75
Lyons Maid Vanilla Kup	85
Lyons Maid Gold Seal Mint Choc Sundae	90
Walls Cornish *or* Blue Ribbon Golden Vanilla Ice Cream Bar	90
Lyons Maid Cornish Raspberry Sundae	95
Lyons Maid Gold Seal Chocolate Nut Sundae	95
Walls Blue Ribbon Golden Vanilla Tub	105
Lyons Maid Cornish Vanilla Kup	110
Lyons Maid Dark Satin Choc Ice	130
Walls Blue Ribbon Dark and Golden Choc Bar	130
Walls Blue Ribbon Golden Vanilla Choc Bar	130

Walls Sundae Cup	130
Lyons Maid Cornish Chocolate Sundae	135
Lyons Maid Cornish Vanilla Choc Ice	125
Walls West Country Cream Vanilla Cup	140
Lyons Maid Twin Choc Ice	150

Canned Fruits in Natural Juice or Low Calorie Syrup

	Calories
Boots Apricots in Low-Calorie Syrup, 220g (7.8 oz)	35
Dietade Apricots, Fruit Salad, Peaches, Pears *or* Pineapple in water, 198g (7 oz)	35
Weight Watchers Fruit Salad, Fruit Cocktail, Peaches *or* Pears in Low-Calorie Syrup, 198g (7 oz)	40
Boots Peaches *or* Pears in Low-Calorie Syrup, 220g (7.8 oz)	45
Boots Fruit Cocktail in Low-Calorie Syrup, 220g (7.8 oz)	50
Weight Watchers Blackberries, Grapefruit, Raspberries *or* Strawberries in Low-Calorie Syrup, 198g (7 oz)	50
Boots Pineapple in Low-Calorie Syrup, 220g (7.8 oz)	55
Weight Watchers Pineapple Rings in Low-Calorie Syrup, 198g (7 oz)	70
Waitrose Grapefruit, Peaches *or* Fruit Cocktail in Natural Juice, 220g (7¾ oz)	75
John West Mandarins in Natural Fruit Juice, 298g (10½ oz)	80
Dietade Fruit Salad in Fruit Sugar Syrup, 227g (8 oz)	90
Koo Fruit Cocktail in Apple Juice, 227g (8 oz)	90

Dietade Apricots *or* Pears in Fruit Sugar Syrup, 227g (8 oz)	95
Koo Peach Slices in Apple Juice, 227g (8 oz)	95
Dietade Pineapple in Fruit Sugar Syrup, 227g (8 oz)	100
Koo Pear Halves in Apple Juice, 227g (8 oz)	105
Sainsbury's Pineapple, Unsweetened, 227g (8 oz)	105
Waitrose Pineapple in Natural Juice, 227g (8 oz)	105
John West Pear Quarters in Natural Fruit Juice, 283g (10 oz)	110
Dietade Peaches in Fruit Sugar Syrup, 227g (8 oz)	115
John West Apricot Halves in Natural Fruit Juice, 283g (10 oz)	115
John West Apple Slices in Natural Fruit Juice, 383g (13$\frac{1}{2}$ oz)	120
John West Grapefruit Segments in Natural Fruit Juice, 283g (10 oz)	120
John West Peach Slices in Natural Juice, 283g (10 oz)	130
John West Pineapple Rings in Natural Juice, 227g (8 oz)	130
John West Fruit Cocktail in Natural Juice, 283g (10 oz)	135
Del Monte Pineapple Slices in Natural Juice, 227g (8 oz)	150
Sainsbury's Apricot Halves, Fruit Cocktail, Peaches *or* Pears in Apple Juice, 411g (14$\frac{1}{2}$ oz)	185

Little Snacks for Nibblers

If you are a nibbler by nature you are unlikely to succeed with your diet if you try to keep to three meals a day. There is no need to stop nibbling entirely if you choose from these very low-calorie snacks.

Save your nibbles for the times when you are most likely to be tempted. It's often not hunger that turns some people to the biscuit tin. Some of us nibble when we are bored or in a stressful situation. Many people nibble in the evening while watching television or before going to bed. If you know there are particularly difficult times for you, it is best to plan ahead and have your nibble readily available. If you can't get through the day at work without picking, try taking one of our low-calorie dips with raw vegetables. If you enjoy a supper-time snack, choose one of our topped crispbreads which can be made in minutes. We have used pickles and chutneys in many of our recipes because we find that a super-strong flavour sensation can often make a small quantity of food surprisingly satisfying. All the following snacks are under 100 calories. If you are a nibbler, just choose one or two snacks a day, deduct the calories from your daily allowance, then decide on what you can afford for your other meals.

It always pays to take care of your dieting weaknesses in advance so they do not strike you unawares.

Beef Paste with Chutney Biscuit
Serves 1: 45 calories

5ml (1 level teaspoon)
 Shiphams Country Pot
 Beef and Pickle Paste
5ml (1 level teaspoon)
 Sharwoods Bengal Hot
 Chutney

1 water biscuit *or* 1 Hovis
 Cracker
cucumber

Spread the biscuit or cracker with the paste and then the chutney. Top with the cucumber.

Sardine and Tomato Biscuit
Serves 1: 45 calories

5ml (1 level teaspoon) sardine spread *or* paste
5ml (1 level teaspoon) tomato chutney
1 water biscuit *or* 1 Hovis cracker

Spread the biscuit or cracker with sardine spread or paste and top with the tomato chutney.

Fruit and Cheese Biscuit
Serves 1: 55 calories

15ml (1 level tablespoon) curd cheese
2 large *or* 4 small grapes
1 water biscuit *or* Hovis cracker

Spread the biscuit or cracker with the curd cheese. Halve the grapes and place on top.

Crab and Relish Crispbread
Serves 1: 65 calories

10ml (2 level teaspoons) crab spread
10ml (2 level teaspoons) cucumber relish
1 Energen *or* Ryvita crispbread

Spread the crispbread with the crab spread (any brand). Top with cucumber relish.

Chicken and Mango Chutney Crispbread
Serves 1: 65 calories

1 Energen *or* Ryvita
  crispbread
10ml (2 level teaspoons)
  chicken spread

10ml (2 level teaspoons)
  mango chutney
cucumber

Spread the crispbread with the chicken spread. Cover with the mango chutney. Top with a few slices of cucumber.

Cottage Cheese and Ham Crispbread
Serves 1: 75 calories

15g (¹/₂ oz) lean ham
1 small gherkin
25g (1 oz) cottage cheese

1 Ryvita *or* Energen
  crispbread

Discard any visible fat from the ham and then chop the lean. Chop the gherkin and mix with the cottage cheese and ham. Spread on the crispbread.

Celery with Fishy Cottage Cheese
Serves 1: 75 calories

2 sticks celery
50g (2 oz) Eden Vale Cottage Cheese with Salmon and
  Cucumber

Wash the celery and fill the hollow part with the cottage
cheese. Cut into short sticks and keep in the refrigerator,
covered with cling film. Take out one piece at a time when
you feel the urge to nibble.

Cheese and Pickle Crispbread
Serves 1: 75 calories

15g (½ oz) Edam cheese
1 Ryvita *or* Energen crispbread
5ml (1 level teaspoon) sweet pickle

Thinly slice or grate the cheese and place on the crispbread.
Top with the pickle.

Ham and Corn Crispbread
Serves 1: 80 calories

1 Energen *or* Ryvita crispbread
10ml (2 level teaspoons) ham spread
10ml (2 level teaspoons) corn relish

Spread the biscuit or cracker with the ham spread and top
with the corn relish.

Cucumber Boats
Serves 1: 80 calories

cucumber
50g (2 oz) cottage cheese with prawns

Use a piece of cucumber about 5cm (2 ins) long, cut in half lengthwise. Scoop out the seeds leaving a hollow channel in the middle. Fill with the cottage cheese with prawns. Cover with cling film and refrigerate until wanted.

Saucy Dip with Vegetables
Serves 1: 80 calories

20ml (4 teaspoons) Worcestershire Sauce
60ml (4 tablespoons) natural yogurt
10ml (2 level teaspoons) tomato purée

2.5ml (½ level teaspoon) English mustard
salt and pepper
50g (2 oz) carrots
50g (2 oz) celery

Mix together the Worcestershire sauce, yogurt, tomato purée and mustard. Season with salt and pepper to taste. Scrub the carrots, wash the celery and then cut both vegetables into bite-sized pieces. Pack the dip in one plastic container and the vegetables in another and either store in the refrigerator or take to work. When you want a nibble, dip a piece of vegetable into the dip.

Little Snacks for Nibblers

Crunchy Cottage Cheese Crispbread
Serves 1: 85 calories

¼ stick celery
1 small gherkin
50g (2 oz) cottage cheese
  with chives

1 Energen *or* Ryvita
  crispbread

Chop the celery and gherkin and mix with the cottage cheese.
Spread on the crispbread.

Celery with Cheese Spread
Serves 1: 85 calories

2 sticks celery
25g (1 oz) Primula Cheese Spread

Wash the celery and then spread the Primula along the
hollow side. Cut into shorter pieces and keep in the
refrigerator, covered with cling film. Take out one piece at
a time when you feel like a nibble.

Stuffed Tomatoes
Serves 1: 85 calories

2 tomatoes
50g (2 oz) St Ivel *or* St Michael Cottage Cheese with Onion
  and Cheddar

Cut the tomatoes in half and using a teaspoon carefully scoop
out the seeds and flesh, leaving the skin intact. Discard the
juice and pips and then chop the flesh and mix with the
cottage cheese. Fill back into the tomato cases.

Sardine and Pickled Onion Crispbread
Serves 1: 95 calories

1 sardine in tomato sauce
1 small pickled onion
2 Energen crispbreads

Mash the sardine. Chop the pickled onion and mix with the sardine. Spread on the crispbread.

Minty Dip with Vegetables
Serves 1: 100 calories

30ml (2 tablespoons) Heinz
  or Waistline Low-Calorie
  Salad Dressing
60ml (4 tablespoons)
  oil-free French dressing

10ml (2 teaspoons)
  concentrated mint sauce
50g (2 oz) carrot
50g (2 oz) cucumber

Mix together the low-calorie salad dressing, oil-free French dressing and concentrated mint sauce. Scrub the carrot and cut into bite-sized pieces with the cucumber. Pack the dip in one plastic container and the vegetables in another and either store in the refrigerator or take to work. When you want a nibble, dip a piece of vegetable into the dip.

Chutney Dip with Vegetables
Serves 1: 100 calories

30ml (2 level tablespoons)
  Sharwoods Bengal Hot
  Chutney
60ml (4 level tablespoons)
  natural yogurt

salt and pepper
50g (2 oz) raw cauliflower
50g (2 oz) cucumber

Mix together the chutney and yogurt and season with salt and pepper. Cut the cauliflower into florets and the cucumber into fingers. Pack the dip in one plastic container and the vegetables in another and either store in the refrigerator or take to work. When you want a nibble, dip a piece of vegetable into the dip.

Curry Dip with Vegetables
Serves 1: 100 calories

30ml (2 level tablespoons) Sharwoods Curry Sauce	salt and pepper
60ml (4 level tablespoons) natural yogurt	50g (2 oz) cucumber
	50g (2 oz) raw cauliflower

Blend the curry sauce and yogurt together and season with salt and pepper. Cut the cucumber into fingers and break the cauliflower into florets. Pack the dip in one plastic container and the vegetables in another and either store in the refrigerator or take to work. When you want a nibble, dip a piece of vegetable into the dip.

Branston Dip with Vegetables
Serves 1: 100 calories

45ml (3 level tablespoons) Branston Spicy Sauce	salt and pepper
45ml (3 level tablespoons) natural yogurt	75g (3 oz) raw carrot
1.25ml (1/4 level teaspoon) Worcestershire sauce	2 sticks celery

Mix together the sauces and yogurt and season with salt and pepper. Scrub the carrot and wash the celery. Pack the dip in one plastic container and the vegetables in another and either store in the refrigerator or take to work. When you want a nibble, dip a piece of vegetable into the dip.

Biscuits

per biscuit	Calories
Quaker Almond Harvest Crunch Bar	80
Quaker Peanut Harvest Crunch Bar	80
Macdonald Taxi	85
Macdonald YoYo, Toffee	85
Jacobs Club Wafer	95
McVitie Bandit	95
McVitie YoYo, Mint *or* Orange	100

Crisps and Savoury Snacks

per smallest packet	Calories
KP Rancheros	60
KP Griddles	75
Walkers Snaps	75
KP Cheesey Crunchies	85
KP Wickers, Chicken *or* Prawn Cocktail	90
Allinson Wheateats	90
Smiths Quavers	95

Soups

	Calories
Campbell's Condensed Soup, Consommé, 295g (10.4 oz)	25
Waistline Low-Calorie Soup, Chicken and Celery, 283g (10 oz)	30
Carnation Slim Soup, per sachet	40
Batchelors Slim-a-Soup, per sachet	40
Knorr Quick Soup, Beef and Onion, per sachet	40
Boots Low-Calorie Soup, Beef and Vegetable, 295g (10.4 oz)	45

Little Snacks for Nibblers

Knorr Quick Soup, Tomato and Beef, per sachet	45
Frank Cooper, Consommé, 425g (15 oz)	50
Waistline Low-Calorie Soup, Golden Vegetable, 283g (10 oz)	50
Knorr Quick Soup, Oxtail, per sachet	50
Knorr Quick Soup, Golden Vegetable, per sachet	55
Waistline Low-Calorie Soup, Tomato *or* Vegetable, 283g (10 oz)	60
Heinz Low-Calorie Soup, Chicken and Vegetable, *or* Scotch Broth, 295g (10.4 oz)	60
Boots Low Calorie Soup, Oxtail *or* Vegetable, 295g (10.4 oz)	65
Campbell's Condensed Soup, Golden Vegetable, 140g (4.9 oz)	65
Waistline Low-Calorie Soup, Oxtail 283g (10 oz)	65
Heinz Low-Calorie Soup, Vegetable, 295g (10.4 oz)	65
Knorr Quick Soup, Tomato and Bacon, per sachet	65
Boots Low-Calorie Soup, Chicken and Vegetable, 295g (10.4 oz)	70
Frank Cooper, French Onion, 425g (15 oz)	70
Heinz Low-Calorie Soup, Chicken *or* Vegetable and Beef, 295g (10.4 oz)	70
Knorr Quick Soup, Chicken, per sachet	70
Crosse and Blackwell Speciality Soups, French Onion, 425g (15 oz)	75
Knorr Quick Soup, Onion, per sachet	75
Heinz Low-Calorie Soup, Tomato, 295g (10.4 oz)	75
Campbell's Condensed Soup, Scotch Broth, 140g (4.9 oz)	100

Yogurts

per individual carton	*Calories*
Safeway Natural	55
Sainsbury's Natural	65

Raines Natural	70
Chambourcy Natural	75
Loseley Natural	75
Waitrose Natural	80
Dessert Farm Apricot	85
St Ivel Natural	85
Safeway Fruit	95
Dessert Farm Natural	100
Sainsbury's Fruit (except Banana, Black Cherry)	100

Eating Out

When you are dieting it is best to keep your eating out to special occasions. It is very difficult to calculate accurately the calories of a portion of restaurant food because of differences in recipes and the amount that is dished up. But there may be days when you would like to meet friends for a lunch-time natter or relax with them over an evening meal. So here we give you a choice of dishes which are always reasonably safe to choose when eating out.

It sometimes seems to us that the restaurant chef and waiters conspire to make our safe choice more fattening. But they aren't entirely to blame, for most catering schools will teach a cook that the customer prefers elaborate fatty sauces with meat or fish, creamy sweet desserts and butter on everything. And isn't that the sort of thing we always used to choose before we started to diet? So as well as giving a list of the safest starters, main meals and desserts, we have also given a few tips on how to keep them reasonable in calories. We have also listed the dishes that must be avoided at all cost. For with these particular recipes there is no chance that you will end up with a meal totalling less than 1300 calories for three courses.

If you would like to include an alcoholic drink with your meal, we give a full list of calorie values on page 152. To make your tipple go further, serve half a glass of wine with half a glass of mineral water. You can drink as much bottled mineral water, ordinary water or low-calorie mixers as you wish. In fact we find that fizzy mineral water sipped during a meal often helps to make us feel full at no extra calorie cost. Pausing to sip water can also slow down your eating. Because it takes about 20 minutes for your body to signal satisfaction, you may eat more than you really need if you gobble your food.

If you are eating out regard it as a treat and try to get satisfaction out of every mouthful of food. It is easy to chat away hardly noticing what you are consuming. So switch your conversation to the food before you while you are eating: 'This melon is deliciously juicy, I'm really enjoying it . . .' and keep other subjects for between courses.

The most dangerous time for a slimmer can be when she goes into a restaurant feeling very hungry. One slimmer we know always eats an apple before she sets off for her lunch-time date. This, she finds, helps stop her being tempted to nibble at buttered rolls while she makes up her mind what to choose from the menu. Remember a buttered roll will cost about 250 calories and it is unlikely that you will be able to afford that and three courses. Of course, if you intend to choose just one course, you could have the roll instead of a starter.

It is usually best to decide what you will eat before you get to a restaurant if that is possible. If you are feeling very hungry when you are choosing from the menu your stomach may overrule your slimming resolve. Many a time hunger has driven us to order a filling starter followed by a main course. Then we have discovered, after the first course, that we would have been perfectly satisfied with that alone.

Try to avoid eating in restaurants where there is a set menu. Not only is it usually impossible to choose a really low-calorie meal, but if you have paid for every course there is the temptation to feel you must eat everything that is put before you.

On days when you eat out, choose a very low-calorie packed lunch or a meal from our selection of low-calorie diet savers.

Starters

The following are the safest starter choices for a slimmer:

Consommé
You can't go wrong with consommé. It is made from beef, stock and vegetables. All the fat (and, therefore, most of the calories) is removed to give the broth its characteristic clarity. You'll pay the highest number of calories for consommé with sherry added – around 55 per serving. If a restaurant serves consommé without sherry your bowlful could be as low as 35 calories. If you accompany your soup with a bread roll, though, you will add about 150 calories and 15g (½ oz) butter will increase your calories by another 105.

Juice
Except for tomato and apple, restaurants almost always serve sweetened juices. Tomato is the lowest fruit juice to choose – less than half the calories of sweetened orange, grapefruit or pineapple. The amount you get could be from about 4 fl. oz to 6 fl. oz. Here is our chart showing calories for three average glasses:

	125ml 4 fl. oz	150ml 5 fl.oz	175ml 6 fl.oz
Orange, sweetened	60	75	90
Grapefruit, sweetened	60	75	90
Pineapple, sweetened	60	75	90
Apple	40	50	60
Tomato	25	30	35

Melon
Again, melon is always a very safe starter choice. An average slice is just 30 calories. Add half a teaspoon of ginger and you won't be adding any calories worth counting. Sprinkle the top with a level teaspoon of sugar and that will increase your starter by 17. Melon is often offered in Italian restaurants accompanied by thinly-sliced Parma ham. Cut off every bit

of fat and the melon and ham could be under 100 calories. But with fatty ham your plateful may increase to 150 calories.

Fresh grapefruit
Half a fresh grapefruit is usually around 20 calories. But most people will not eat grapefruit without some sort of sweetener. Some restaurants now offer sugar substitutes which will sweeten your grapefruit for few calories. Two level teaspoons of sugar, at 35 calories, will cost almost twice as much as the grapefruit. Half a glacé cherry tops your grapefruit with another 5 calories. Unless you go mad on the sugar, though, it would be hard to make this starter more than 60 calories.

Grapefruit Cocktail
If a restaurant serves grapefruit cocktail it will almost certainly be made from tinned grapefruit segments in syrup served with a glacé cherry. Calories will depend on the size of portions and could be from about 55 calories to 90 calories.

Oysters
Count about 5 calories per oyster if served raw with a squeeze of lemon. Even if the oysters are fried in butter, your half dozen will only increase from 30 calories to about 70. But don't eat the accompanying bread and butter unless you want to increase your starter by about 160 calories.

Smoked Salmon
An expensive dish and restaurants tend not to be overgenerous in servings. A generous portion would be about 50g (2 oz) which will total 80 calories. Again, just one round of brown bread and butter will add 160 calories.

Starters to avoid
All the following are usually over 300 calories a portion and are too calorie-costly to be followed by another course. So

make a note to avoid them when choosing a starter. However, many restaurants are willing to serve a starter as a main course and the pasta dishes, in particular, are often quite large enough to eat as a single-course lunch and will usually cost under 400 calories.

Avocado Vinaigrette
Avocado with Prawns *or* other Seafood
Cannelloni
Lasagne
Spaghetti Bolognese
Fried Whitebait
Scallops Mornay
Pâté with Toast
Taramasalata with Pitta Bread *or* Toast

Main Courses

Now the task of making the best choice becomes much more difficult. Restaurants vary enormously in their portion sizes and recipes. However, we have chosen thirteen dishes which you can safely rely on to be between 300 and 400 calories a portion. A good basic rule when eating out is to say 'No' to butter on anything. Just a 1/2-oz knob will add 105 calories to any dish.

Braised Kidneys
Kidneys are always a good diet choice. For even if the chef decides to fry them before he braises, they won't absorb much of the fat which can add hundreds of calories to any dish. Choose green vegetables to accompany your braised kidneys and tell the waiter to serve them plain without butter.

Calves Liver in Wine Sauce

A favourite recipe in many Italian restaurants. Liver is reasonable in calories, supplies many essential nutrients and is always a good choice for slimmers. If the wine sauce is served separately have as small a portion as you can manage, for this is where most of the calories lurk. Accompany your calves liver with plain green vegetables or a small portion of boiled rice.

Grilled Dover Sole

The chef will always grill Dover sole with butter to stop it drying and some of these fatty calories are absorbed by the fish. But you can save lots of extra calories by asking that it be served plain without extra butter. As most chefs dislike serving anything plain, you may have to repeat this request when the waiter arrives with your fish swimming in a buttery sea. But persevere and tell him to take it away and drain off the fat. Eventually the message will filter through to the kitchens – remember the customer is always right. You could probably afford to have a couple of plain boiled potatoes with your fish plus green vegetables. It is also good served with a salad – no dressing, of course.

Herb or Plain Omelette

Not all omelettes are safe for slimmers. Cheese is costly calorie-wise and mushrooms are usually fried which increases them from 4 calories an ounce to 50 calories an ounce. A three-egg plain or herb omelette will probably be around 300 calories and makes a good lunchtime choice if served with a plain salad. Tomato omelettes are usually another safe bet as the tomato is not fried.

Roast Beef and Gravy

Portion sizes of any roast meat vary enormously from restaurant to restaurant – usually the more you pay the more you get. If you are eating in a carvery, don't cut yourself more than two slices, and cut them as thin as possible. It is always a big calorie saving if you cut off as much fat as you can and leave it at the side of your plate. If you keep your gravy to a minimum (likely to be fatty) you could probably afford to choose between a Yorkshire Pudding or two roast potato chunks to add to your plain vegetables.

Roast or Grilled Chicken

If you don't eat the skin off a chicken leg you can save approximately 100 calories. And always ask for a small portion of stuffing if this is offered. Unless it is fried in egg and breadcrumbs, chicken is always a good choice for slimmers. Grilled chicken can be accompanied with a plain salad and roast chicken with gravy and vegetables.

Lamb Kebabs

Lamb kebabs, or souvlaki as they may be called in a Greek restaurant, are a reasonably safe diet choice and differences in calories will mostly come from portion sizes. The lamb is marinaded in oil, lemon and herbs before being threaded on skewers with onion, mushrooms and perhaps peppers. Lamb kebabs are not often served with a sauce and the best accompaniment is plain boiled rice.

Steak Tartare

Not to everyone's taste this dish – a mixture of minced raw steak, egg yolk and seasoning, sometimes garnished with anchovies and hardboiled egg. Calories, again, will vary according to size of portion. A minimum 4-oz portion will cost about 200 calories and for each extra ounce of steak that is served onto your plate, you pay about 35 calories. Steak Tartare is best served with an undressed salad.

Grilled steak

Many steak bars now sell steaks which weigh no more than 175g (6 oz) and these are the best to choose if you are counting your calories. Another factor to note is that the more you cook a steak, the lower in calories it becomes because extra

113

fat drips away. We show in the table below the calorie variations for average-size steaks usually served in steak bars and restaurants. To accompany your steak choose a salad without dressing (ask for this when you order or it may arrive covered in oily French dressing). A potato baked in its jacket (without butter) would be an extra 250 calories; a portion of french fries 400!

Steak	175g (6 oz)	225g (8 oz)	275g (10 oz)
Well done	260	345	435
Medium	290	385	485
Rare	310	415	515

Grilled Lobster
Lobster is brushed with oil before grilling and may be served with melted butter or a sauce. A small whole lobster weighs approximately 375g (13 oz) and is about 155 calories before grilling. All additional calories will come from the amount of fat it is cooked or served in. Remember that just 25g (1 oz) butter will add 210 calories to your dish. Grilled lobster can be eaten with a mixed undressed salad. Refuse all offer of mayonnaise which will cost you 95 calories for a level tablespoon.

Cold Meat Salads
An average portion of cold meat served with a salad in a restaurant will be 125g (4 oz). If you choose ham, beef or pork, the highest you are likely to pay is 325 calories a serving. But you can reduce this figure considerably by just cutting off the fat and leaving it at the side of your plate. We found we could cut 80 calories from a portion of ham; 70 calories from a portion of beef and 100 calories from a portion of roast pork. Make sure the salad your meat is served with is made of fresh greens, tomatoes or onions. If you are also served a dollop of mayonnaise-covered potato salad, cole-

slaw, corn salad or some oily rice or pasta salad, then leave it behind with the fat from your meat.

Prawn Salad

Chefs love to cover this deliciously low-calorie seafood with high-calorie sauce. Seafood sauce, unless it is the Waistline variety not usually stocked by restaurants, is always high in calories. Your best plan is to find out before you order if the prawns are plain. If they arrive on your plate covered in sauce, there is no way you can avoid eating it. Grilled prawns, which are normally the large Pacific or Butterfly sorts, will probably be grilled in butter, but if they are served plain are a better bet than prawns in seafood sauce.

Hamburgers

A small hamburger in a bun is not usually more than 300 calories wherever it is served. So this can be a good lunch-time choice as long as you can resist ordering chips to eat with it. A portion of chips could add about 290 calories. You wouldn't save much by having a portion of coleslaw at about 200 calories. If your local hamburger joint does serve plain salads, then you can have as many of these as you like with your burger, plus your choice from the relish rack. Beware bigger burgers, though. A quarter-pounder costs about 550 calories and a half-pounder could come to almost 1000 calories. We have even discovered one hamburger joint that serves pound burgers – don't even think about ordering one!

Main courses to avoid

These main courses are almost always over 600 calories a portion, so never, ever order them.

Beef Curry with Rice	Chicken Chasseur
Beef Stroganoff with Rice *or* Noodles	Chicken Marengo
	Chicken Pie

Coq au Vin
Duck in Orange Sauce
Lamb Curry with Rice
Lamb Cutlet *en Croûte*
Lasagne
Moussaka

Paella
Sole *Meunière*
Spaghetti Bolognese
Steak and Kidney Pie
Steak Diane
Tournedos Rossini

Desserts

Some people, we find, are passionately fond of desserts and can hardly take their eyes off the sweet trolley while they are sitting in a restaurant. Other people eat a dessert because they have got into the habit of having something sweet to finish a meal. If you belong to the first group, you *must* choose a dessert or you will end up feeling deprived and feel that you haven't enjoyed your meal at all. In this case try to keep your other courses as low in calories as you can so you can spend most of your calories on what you really desire. If you belong to the second group your best long-term plan is to gradually get into the habit of saying 'No', if you really are no longer hungry when you have finished your main course. If you do eat dessert, the following are the safest choices for a slimmer. None of them will usually add up to more than 200 calories – unless you add cream.

Fresh Fruit
We give a complete list of the calorie values of fresh fruit on page 138. This is always the safest choice of all in a restaurant and even if you choose a large banana it won't come to more than 95 calories.

Fresh Fruit Salad
Although fruit salad on its own is never high in calories, sugar or syrup bases add calories to the otherwise innocent fruit. Restaurants will usually make fruit salads with syrup to prevent the fruit browning and often they add wine for

flavour. An average portion, though, is not likely to be more than 150 calories. You can save a few calories if you leave the syrup in your dish. Refuse all offers of cream which can add up to 250 calories for double or 125 for single.

Fresh Pineapple with Kirsch

A restaurant will slice up a whole pineapple or two, and soak the slices in Kirsch. How much liqueur your slice absorbs may depend on if it is served from the top of the bowl or the bottom! If you get a whole 2ml (⅙ gill) measure of Kirsch on your pineapple, though, the calorie cost would not be above 100 calories. And as the Kirsch sweetens as well as preserves, the restaurant is unlikely to add additional sugar – although you are likely to be offered cream (waiters seem willing to pour this on practically anything, we find).

Lychees

This Chinese delicacy is a welcome sight on any menu – it offers a luxury taste for under 20 calories an ounce. The lychees most probably will be canned rather than fresh, but unlike other canned fruit, lychees don't need custard or cream; either would spoil the delicate flavour. As lychees are a costly fruit, portions are usually fairly small and shouldn't be above 90 calories (for about seven lychees).

Fruit Sorbet

A sorbet is merely iced water with flavouring and a little sugar, so it's always a safe choice wherever you are eating. A small restaurant scoop gives you just 40g (1½ oz) – a mere 50 calories' worth of sorbet. Even if the restaurant serves a double scoop, sorbet is still one of the lowest calorie desserts. There are little calorie differences between the flavours which are usually orange, lemon or raspberry.

Baked Egg Custard

Probably only available on the more 'homely' menus. Made from a mixture of milk, eggs and a little sugar and nutmeg, an individual egg custard won't be above 200 calories. In expensive restaurants there is the possibility, however, that the chef may sneakily add cream to the basic mixture to make a richer pud. When in doubt, choose another dessert.

Crème Caramel

Though the sugar, eggs and milk from which this dessert is made are all rather high-calorie, it is usually baked in small individual dishes. An average crème caramel will be about 200 calories – although this could rise to about 235 calories if cream is added to the custard mixture.

Ice Cream

Despite its name, ice cream – even the dairy variety – is much lower in calories than many people imagine. And the ingredients are whisked to trap in lots of no-calorie air! Ice cream averages out at around 50 calories an ounce. The average restaurant serving of two scoops is generous; and with a wafer, your ice cream dessert will come to 155 calories. You could even afford to add a scoop of ice cream to your strawberries or raspberries instead of the usual cream.

Zabaglione

A delicious mix of eggs, sugar and sherry which is whisked up so that it is light and frothy. It is entirely due to the fact that your glass of Zabaglione contains a large percentage of non-calorie air that this dessert is usually a surprisingly low 150 to 200 calories a portion. Ask the waiter to serve it without the usual biscuits, however. Just one finger of shortbread would bump your calories up by about 100. If you not only crave something sweet but also like something alcoholic to finish a meal, Zabaglione can meet two desires with one dessert.

Desserts to avoid

An average portion of any of these puds would be over 400 calories. Some are stodgy and fairly obviously high in calories, but others, such as syllabub, seem reasonably innocent because they slip down so easily. Make a mental note never to choose these desserts when you are eating out.

Apple Dumpling and Custard
Flapjack and Syrup
Jam Roly-Poly and Custard
Jam Sponge and Custard
Chocolate Profiteroles
Crème Brûlée
Rum Baba
Spotted Dick and Custard
Syllabub
Syrup Sponge and Custard

Diet Menus

Start your diet by following some of the menus given here. Once you have the idea, you can make up your own menus using the recipes and calorie charts given in this book. If you have just a few pounds to lose keep to a strict 1000 calories a day; or if your problem is a weightier one, then you can pick from either the 1250-or 1500-calorie menus. Learn to be realistic about how you are likely to cope with dieting. If you know you are going to be eating out, there is a special day's menu on page 136. Or follow the eating out advice which starts on page 107. You may not lose much weight on that day but you certainly won't gain any. And that is good. If you are on one of the higher calorie menus and you have a little slip, don't worry. Next day you can choose a 1000-calorie menu and your weight loss will continue as planned.

Always measure out your milk allowance into a jug each morning. It is almost impossible to keep a check on how much milk you are using if you just tip it into your coffee or tea cup. Skimmed milk is widely available in bottles or cartons, but if you do have any difficulty getting it you can make up a supply using low-fat powdered milk such as Marvel. Be careful, though, that the powdered milk you buy is labelled 'low-fat'. Some powdered milks are higher in calories.

We have called the first meal of the day breakfast. But if you don't normally eat breakfast, you can save this meal until later in the day. You can eat any of the meals at any time of the day that you wish; it is the total number of calories you eat in the day that is important, not when you eat them. If your menu allows you a snack or nibble, save these for the times when you know you are most likely to need them.

Variety is the basis of good nutrition, so don't stick to the same menu all the time. In order to ensure that you get a supply of all essential vitamins and nutrients you should follow at least seven different menus during a month.

There is no need to restrict liquids on a diet, unless they contain calories. Black coffee, tea and water are all calorie free. You can also drink as much as you like of soft drinks labelled low-calorie and Bovril, Marmite or yeast extract drinks. These contain so few calories, they're not worth counting.

Now choose your menu and get out a pen and some paper. Write down all the ingredients you are going to need for the next few days. Shop today – and tomorrow you can take the first step towards your new slim future.

1000 Calories

Milk Allowance
275ml (½ pint) skimmed milk to use in tea or coffee throughout the day.

Breakfast
All-Bran with Dried Apricots (page 15)

Packed Lunch
Watercress and Curd Cheese Sandwich (page 34)
1 large orange

Main Meal
Spicy Grilled Fish (page 52)
1 Eden Vale Syllabub

Milk Allowance
275ml (¹/₂ pint) skimmed milk to use in drinks throughout the day.

Breakfast
Marmalade *or* Jam and Toast (page 16)

Packed Lunch
Egg Salad (page 31)

Main Meal
Moussaka with Tomato Salad (page 68)
Baked Apple with Mincemeat (page 85)

Milk Allowance
275ml (¹/₂ pint) skimmed milk to use in tea and coffee throughout the day.

Breakfast
Bacon and Tomatoes (page 17)

Packed Lunch
Fruit and Nut Slaw (page 34)

Main Meal
Liver Casserole with Pasta (page 57)
1 Eden Vale Strawberry Fool

Diet Menus

Milk Allowance
275ml (¹/₂ pint) skimmed milk to use in tea and coffee throughout the day.

Breakfast
2 Weetabix
5ml (1 level teaspoon) sugar
125ml (4 fl. oz) skimmed milk (extra to allowance)

Packed Lunch
Spicy Chicken Sandwich with Fruit (page 32)

Main Meal
Beef Curry, Rice and Cucumber Salad (page 66)

Snack
2 Ham and Corn Crispbreads (page 99)

Milk Allowance
275ml (¹/₂ pint) skimmed milk to use in tea and coffee throughout the day.

Breakfast
Cottage Cheese and Ham Sandwich (page 24)

Packed Lunch
Soup, Yogurt and Fruit (page 33)

Main Meal
Curried Chicken Salad (page 45)
Blackberry Baked Apple (page 84), served with 30ml (2 tablespoons) natural yogurt

Nibbles
Sardine and Pickled Onion Crispbreads (page 102)

Milk Allowance
275ml (¹/₂ pint skimmed milk) to use in tea and coffee throughout the day.

Breakfast
Yogurt with Wheatgerm and Raisins (page 22)

Packed Lunch
Cheese, Ham and Fruit Salad (page 37)

Main Meal
Sausages, Bacon and Beans (page 65)
1 Lyons Maid Cornish Vanilla Kup *or* 1 Chambourcy Tropical Fruit Sundae

Milk Allowance
275ml (¹/₂ pint) skimmed milk to use in tea and coffee throughout the day.

Breakfast
Crispbreads with Cheese Spread (page 21)

Packed Lunch
Instant Lunch and Fruit (page 40)

Afternoon Nibble
Small packet Sainsbury's Ready Salted Crisps *or* Walkers
French Fries

Main Meal
Cod in Shrimp Sauce with Vegetable Rice (page 58)
1 small banana

Milk Allowance
275ml (½ pint) skimmed milk to use in tea and coffee
throughout the day.

Breakfast
Poached Egg on Toast (page 16)

Lunch
Cauliflower Cheese (page 77)
1 medium apple

Main Meal
Fish and Tomato Pie (page 54)
Rice Pudding with Sultanas (page 88)

1250 Calories

Milk Allowance
275ml (¹/₂ pint) skimmed milk to use in tea and coffee throughout the day.

Breakfast
Bran Flakes *or* Special K with Raisins (page 15)

Packed Lunch
Cheese and Pineapple Salad (page 38)

Main Meal
Spicy Pork and Pepper Pot (page 48)
50g (2 oz) long-grain rice, boiled
Pears Belle Hélène (page 88)

Nibbles
Chicken and Mango Chutney Crispbread (page 98)

Milk Allowance
275ml (¹/₂ pint) skimmed milk to use in tea and coffee throughout the day.

Breakfast
Bacon and Baked Beans (page 18)

Packed Lunch
Cottage Cheese and Savoury Snacks with Fruit (page 39)

Diet Menus

Afternoon Snack
1 Prewett's Muesli Fruit Dessert Bar

Main Meal
Chicken and Cauliflower Curry with Rice (page 65)
Banana, Nut and Yogurt Dessert (page 90)

Milk Allowance
275ml (¹/₂ pint) skimmed milk to use in tea and coffee
throughout the day.

Breakfast
Porridge with Honey (page 17)

Nibble
Branston Dip with Vegetables (page 103)

Packed Lunch
Sardine and Olive Sandwich (page 38)
1 large orange

Main Meal
Braised Liver with Vegetables (page 55)
1 Eden Vale Black Cherry *or* Strawberry Cheesecake

Milk Allowance
275ml (¹/₂ pint) skimmed milk to use in tea and coffee
throughout the day.

Breakfast
Citrus Yogurt with Raisins (page 24)

Packed Lunch
Fruity, Carrot and Cheese Salad (page 36)

Sweet Nibble
1 Rowntree Mackintosh Texan

Main Meal
Eggy Smoked Haddock (page 58)
Banana and Custard (page 87)

Milk Allowance
275ml (½ pint) skimmed milk to use in tea and coffee throughout the day.

Breakfast
1 Prewett's Fruit and Nut Dessert Bar
1 small carton St Ivel Natural Yogurt

Packed Lunch
Chicken and Corn Relish Sandwich (page 36)
1 medium banana

Main Meals
Cheesy Egg and Prawns (page 49)
Honey-poached Pear (page 83)
1 Lyons Maid Vanilla Bar

Diet Menus

Snack
1 small packet KP Discos

Milk Allowance
275ml (¹/₂ pint) milk to use in tea and coffee throughout the day.

Breakfast
Egg and Marmite Sandwich (page 25)

Packed Lunch
Coleslaw with Chicken (page 32)
1 St Ivel Trifle *or* 1 Eden Vale Chocolate *or* Fruit Fresh Cream Dessert

Main Meal
Special Macaroni Cheese (page 62)
Fresh Fruit Jelly (page 87)

Milk Allowance
275ml (¹/₂ pint) skimmed milk to use in tea and coffee throughout the day.

Breakfast
Yogurt and Banana (page 23)

Packed Lunch
Rice Quick Lunch Plus Fruit (page 35)

Afternoon Snack
1 small pack Golden Wonder, KP *or* Smiths Crisps

Main Meal
Tuna and Tomato Bake (page 44)
Choc Bar with Tangy Orange Sauce (page 89)

Evening Snack
Savoury Grilled Toast (page 72)

Milk Allowance
275ml (½ pint) skimmed milk to use in tea and coffee
throughout the day.

Breakfast
Bacon Sandwich (page 20)

Lunch
Savoury Pancakes with Grilled Tomatoes (page 77)
1 large orange

Main Meal
Bean and Mince Stew (page 56)
175g (6 oz) potato, baked in its jacket and topped with 15ml
(1 level tablespoon) natural yogurt
Apricot Mousse (page 84)

1500 Calories

Milk Allowance
275ml (¹/₂ pint) skimmed milk to use in tea and coffee throughout the day.

Breakfast
Scrambled Eggs on Toast (page 19)

Packed Lunch
Salmon and Corn Salad (page 41)
1 medium apple

Sweet Snack
1 Rowntree Mackintosh Drifter *or* Cadbury's Picnic

Main Meal
Beef Risotto (page 68)
Snack Size can Ambrosia Rice Pudding, 170g (6 oz)

Milk Allowance
275ml (¹/₂ pint) skimmed milk for use in tea and coffee throughout the day.

Breakfast
Wholemeal Toast and Marmalade *or* Honey (page 19)

Packed Lunch
Cottage Cheese, Crisps and Fruit (page 41)

Sweet Snack
1 Rowntree Mackintosh Toffee Crisp

Main Meal
Stuffed Pork Chop with Vegetables (page 57)
227-g (8-oz) can Del Monte Pineapple Slices in Natural Juice
1 Lyons Maid Vanilla Bar

Evening Snack
1 Findus Toasted Sandwich, Beef *or* Ham and Cheese, cooked as instructed without any added fat

Milk Allowance
275ml (1/2 pint) skimmed milk to use in tea and coffee throughout the day.

Breakfast
Muesli (page 20)

Packed Lunch
Cheese and Pickle Crusty Roll (page 42)
1 large banana

Main Meal
Meat Pudding with Carrots (page 52)
1/2 packet Yeoman Creamy Mashed Potato, made up without butter
1 carton St Ivel Countess Yogurt

Evening Nibble
1 Chicken and Mango Chutney Crispbread (page 98)

Milk Allowance
275ml (½ pint) skimmed milk for use in tea and coffee throughout the day.

Breakfast
Cheese on Toast (page 18)

Packed Lunch
Chicken, Pineapple and Pepper Sandwich (page 40)
1 small carton Ski Yogurt, any flavour
1 large orange

Main Meal
Plaice and Chips (page 68)
1 Ross Mousse Cup, any flavour

Evening Snack
Banana and Bacon Toast (page 74)

Milk Allowance
275ml (½ pint) skimmed milk to use in tea and coffee throughout the day.

Breakfast
Crispbreads with Liver Sausage and Tomatoes (page 25)

Packed Lunch
Barbecued Chicken Sandwich (page 35)
150g (5 oz) grapes

Main Meal
French Bread Pizza with Coleslaw (page 67)
1 Eden Vale Strawberry Fool

Evening Treat
2 glasses dry *or* medium white wine, 125ml (4 fl. oz) each *or* 75ml (3 single measures) whisky *or* gin *or* vodka with low-calorie mixers
1 small packet Golden Wonder *or* KP *or* Smiths crisps

Milk Allowance
275ml (¹/₂ pint) skimmed milk to use in tea and coffee throughout the day.

Breakfast
1 Jordan's Original Crunchy Bar with Honey and Almonds
1 large orange

Packed Lunch
Pâté with Crispbreads and Tomato (page 42)
1 large banana

Sweet Treat
1 Cadbury's Milk Chocolate Flake, 34g

Main Meal
Fruity Baconburgers with Vegetables (page 67)
1 small carton St Michael Muesli Yogurt

Milk Allowance
275ml (¹/₂ pint) skimmed milk to use in tea and coffee throughout the day.

Breakfast
Shredded Wheat (page 20)

Packed Lunch
Garlic Sausage and Baked Bean Salad (page 40)
150g (5 oz) grapes

Main Meal
Mixed Grill with Spaghetti (page 68)
Peach Melba (page 85)

Evening Snack
Soup with Bread (page 80)

Milk Allowance
275ml (¹/₂ pint) skimmed milk to use in tea and coffee throughout the day.

Breakfast
Bacon Sandwich (page 20)

Lunch
Chunky Soup Meal (page 47)

Main Meal
Roast Chicken Dinner (page 66)
Baked Apricot Custard (page 89)

Evening Treat
2 glasses medium *or* dry white wine, 125ml (4 fl. oz) each *or*
3 single measures whisky *or* gin *or* vodka, 25ml (¹/₆ gill)
each
1 small packet Golden Wonder *or* KP *or* Smiths Crisps

Milk Allowance
275ml (¹/₂ pint) skimmed milk to use in tea and coffee
throughout the day.

Breakfast
Weetabix (page 17)

Packed Lunch
Cottage Cheese, Crispbreads and Celery (page 32)

Restaurant Meal
Melon *or* fresh grapefruit without sugar
Rump Steak, medium *or* well-grilled, 225g (8 oz) raw
(remove large pieces of fat before eating)
Mustard
Large baked jacket potato, without butter *or* sour cream
Mixed Salad without dressing
Ice Cream (without sauce, cream or nuts), *or* Fresh
strawberries *or* raspberries (without cream)
Coffee with milk (not cream) and no sugar
¹/₂ bottle wine

Calorie Charts

BASIC FOODS

Vegetables

	Calories
Asparagus, per spear	4
Aubergine, raw, per 25g (1 oz)	4
Aubergine, average whole aubergine, 200g (7 oz)	30
Baked Beans in Tomato Sauce, per 150-g (5.3-oz) can	110
Baked Beans in Tomato Sauce per 225-g (7.9-oz) can	160
Bean Sprouts, raw per 25g (1 oz)	5
Beetroot, boiled, per 25g (1 oz)	12
Broad Beans, boiled, per 25g (1 oz)	14
Broccoli, raw, per 25g (1 oz)	7
Brussels Sprouts, raw, per 25g (1 oz)	7
Butter Beans, per 223-g (7.9-oz) can	150
Cabbage, raw, per 25g (1 oz)	6
Carrots, raw, per 25g (1 oz)	6
Cauliflower, raw, per 25g (1 oz)	4
Celery, per stick	5
Courgettes, per average courgette	10
Courgettes, per average courgette, slice and fried	40
Cucumber, per 25g (1 oz)	3
Leeks, per average whole leek	25
Lettuce, per 25g (1 oz)	3
Mushrooms, raw per 25g (1 oz)	4
Mushrooms, 50g (2 oz) raw weight, sliced and fried	100

Mustard and Cress, per whole carton	5
Onions, per average small onion	15
Onions, fried, per 15ml (1 level tablespoon)	25
Onion, pickled, each	5
Onion, spring, each	5
Parsnips, raw, per 25g (1 oz)	14
Peas, Frozen, per 25g (1 oz)	15
Peas, mushy, per 304-g (10.7-oz) can	245
Peppers, per average red *or* green pepper	20
Potatoes, raw, per 25g (1 oz)	25
Potatoes, canned, new potatoes, drained, per 25g (1 oz)	20
Potato chips, average thickness, per average portion, 150g (5 oz)	350
Potatoes, oven chips, per 25g (1 oz)	45
Potatoes, roast, per medium chunk, 45g (1¾ oz)	75
Potato, mashed with a little milk and butter, per average portion, 150g (5 oz)	170
Potato, dry instant mash, per 15ml (1 level tablespoon)	40
Red Kidney Beans, per 223-g (7.9-oz) can	165
Radishes, each	2
Sweetcorn, frozen per 25g (1 oz)	25
Sweetcorn, canned, per 198-g (7-oz) can	154
Runner beans, raw or frozen, per 25g (1 oz)	7
Tomatoes, each, raw	10
Tomatoes, per 227-g (8-oz) can	25
Watercress, per 25g (1 oz)	4

Fruit

Apples, per small eating apple	35
Apples, per medium eating apple	50
Apples, per large eating apple	70
Apple, per medium cooking apple	80
Apricots, per average raw fruit	7

Apricots, per average dried apricot	10
Apricots, canned in natural juice, per 25g (1 oz)	13
Avocado, per average half	235
Banana, per small banana	65
Banana, per medium banana	80
Banana, per large banana	95
Blackberries, raw, per 25g (1 oz)	8
Blackcurrants, raw, per 25g (1 oz)	8
Cherries, fresh with stones, per 25g (1 oz)	12
Cherries, glacé, each	10
Currants, per 15ml (1 level tablespoon)	25
Currants, per 25g (1 oz)	69
Dates, dried with stones, per 25g (1 oz)	60
Dates, fresh with stones, per 25g (1 oz)	30
Dates, fresh, each	15
Gooseberries, fresh ripe dessert, per 25g (1 oz)	10
Gooseberries, fresh cooking, per 25g (1 oz)	5
Grapefruit, per average half	20
Grapefruit canned in natural juice, per 25g (1 oz)	11
Grapes, black, per 25g (1 oz)	14
Grapes, white, per 25g (1 oz)	17
Kiwi Fruit, per medium fruit	30
Lychees, canned per 25g (1 oz)	19
Mandarins, each	20
Melon, Cantaloupe *or* Honeydew *or* Yellow, per average slice, 225g (8 oz)	30
Orange, per small orange	35
Orange, per medium orange	55
Orange, per large orange	75
Peaches, per medium fresh peach	35
Peaches, per large fresh peach	55
Peaches, canned in natural juice, per 25g (1 oz)	13
Peaches, per peach half canned in syrup, drained	25
Pears, per medium fresh pear	40
Pears, canned in natural juice, per 25g (1 oz)	11
Pineapple, canned in natural juice, per 25g (1 oz)	15
Pineapple, fresh, per 25g (1 oz)	13

Plums, fresh dessert plums with stones, per 25g
(1 oz)   10
Plums, per medium Victoria dessert plum   15
Prunes, each   10
Raisins, per 25g (1 oz)   70
Raisins, per 15ml (1 level tablespoon)   25
Raspberries, fresh *or* frozen, per 25g (1 oz)   7
Rhubarb, raw, per 25g (1 oz)   2
Strawberries, fresh *or* frozen, per 25g (1 oz)   7
Sultanas, per 25g (1 oz)   71
Sultanas, per 15ml (1 level tablespoon)   25
Tangerines, each   20
Watermelon, per slice, 225g (8 oz)   25

Meat and Poultry

Bacon

1 back rasher, well-grilled   80
1 streaky rasher, well-grilled   50
1 bacon steak, well-grilled, 100g (3½ oz) raw   105

Beef
Ground beef, very lean, raw, per 25g (1 oz)   45
Ground beef, very lean, fried and drained of fat,
25g (1 oz) raw weight   40
Minced beef, raw, per 25g (1 oz) raw   63
Minced beef, fried and drained of fat, 25g
(1 oz) raw weight   45
Sirloin, roast, lean and fat, per 25g (1 oz)   80
Sirloin, roast, lean only, per 25g (1 oz)   55
Topside, roast, lean and fat, per 25g (1 oz)   61
Topside, roast lean only, per 25g (1 oz)   44
Stewing Steak, raw, lean only, per 25g (1 oz)   35
Rump steak, well-grilled, 170g (6 oz) raw   260
Rump steak, medium-grilled, 170g (6 oz) raw   290

Calorie Charts

Rump steak, rare-grilled, 170g (6 oz) raw	310

Chicken

Roast meat, no skin, per 25g (1 oz)	42
Roast meat and skin, per 25g (1 oz)	61
Breast fillet, raw, no skin, per 25g (1 oz)	34
Whole chicken breast, grilled, 175g (6 oz) raw weight	200
Whole chicken breast, grilled and skin removed, 175g (6 oz) raw weight	145
Chicken drumstick, grilled, 100g (3½ oz) raw weight	85
Chicken drumstick, grilled and skin removed, 100g (3½ oz) raw weight	65
Chicken leg joint, grilled, 225g (8 oz) raw weight	250
Chicken leg joint, grilled and skin removed, 225g (8 oz) raw weight	165
Chicken leg joint, poached in stock and skin removed, 225g (8 oz) raw weight	165

Duck

Roast, meat only	54
Roast, meat and skin	96

Lamb

Leg, roast, lean only, without bone	54
Leg, roast, lean and fat, without bone	76
Chump chop, well grilled, 150g (5 oz) raw weight	205
Loin chop, well grilled, 150g (5 oz) raw weight	175

Kidneys

All types raw, per 25g (1 oz)	25
Lamb's kidney, grilled without fat, each	50
Lamb's kidney, fried, each	65

Liver

Chicken, raw, per 25g (1 oz)	38
Lambs, raw, per 25g (1 oz)	51
Pigs, raw, per 25g (1 oz)	44
Ox, raw, per 25g (1 oz)	46

Pork

Fillet, raw, lean only	42
Leg, raw, lean only, without bone	42
Leg, roast, lean only, without bone	53
Leg, roast, lean and fat, without bone	81
Crackling, average portion, 10g (1/3 oz)	65
Pork chop, well-grilled, 185g (6½ oz) raw	240

Sausages
each

Beef chipolata, well-grilled	50
Beef sausage, well-grilled	120
Pork chipolata, well-grilled	65
Pork sausage, well-grilled	125
Pork and beef chipolata, well-grilled	60
Pork and beef large, well-grilled	125

Turkey
per 25g (1 oz)

Meat only, raw	30
Meat only, roast	40
Meat and skin, roast	49

Veal

Fillet, raw, per 25g (1 oz)	31
Escalope fried in egg and breadcrumbs, 75g (3 oz) raw weight	310

Calorie Charts

Cooked Meat and Delicatessen Sausages
per 25g (1 oz)

Bierwurst	75
Bockwurst	180
Cervelat	140
Chopped ham roll *or* loaf	75
Corned beef	62
Frankfurter	78
Garlic sausage	70
Ham, boiled, lean only	47
Ham, boiled, fatty	90
Kabanos	115
Liver sausage	88
Mortadella, Italian	105
Polony	80
Pork boiling ring	110
Salami, Danish	160
Salami, Hungarian	130
Salami, German	120
Saveloy	74
Tongue, lamb's, stewed	82

Fish
per 25g (1 oz) unless otherwise stated

Cod, fillet, raw	22
Cod fillet, in batter, fried	57
Coley, fillet, raw	21
Crab, meat only	36
Crab, per whole average crab	95
Fish cake, average, grilled without added fat, each	60
Fish finger, average, grilled without fat, each	50
Haddock, fillet, raw	21
Haddock, smoked fillet, steamed *or* poached in water	29
Halibut, cutlet, on the bone, raw	26
Herring, on the bone, grilled	38

Herring, whole herring, grilled, 135g (4½ oz) raw weight	170
Herring rollmop, each	120
Kipper, fillet, baked *or* grilled	58
Kipper, whole kipper with bones, grilled, 175g (6 oz) raw weight	280
Mackerel, fillet, raw	63
Mackerel, kippered	62
Mackerel, smoked	70
Mackerel, whole raw mackerel, 225g (8 oz)	318
Oysters, each	5
Pilchards, canned in tomato sauce	36
Plaice, fillet, raw *or* steamed	26
Plaice, whole fillet in breadcrumbs, fried, 170g (6 oz) raw weight	435
Prawns, shelled	30
Sardines, per average sardine canned in oil, drained	62
Sardines, per average sardine canned in tomato sauce, drained	50
Shrimps, canned, drained	27
Shrimps, fresh, without shells	33
Sole, fillet, raw	23
Trout, whole trout, poached *or* grilled without fat, 175g (6 oz) raw	150
Whole smoked trout, 155g (5½ oz)	150
Tuna, canned in brine, per 100-g (3½-oz) can	110
Tuna, canned in brine, drained, per 25g (1 oz)	30
Tuna, canned in oil, per 100-g (3½-oz) can	285
Tuna, canned in oil, drained, per 25g (1 oz)	60
Whitebait, fried	149
Whiting, fillet, steamed	26

Eggs
per egg

Size 1, raw	95
Size 1, fried	115
Size 2, raw	90

Size 2, fried	110
Size 3, raw	80
Size 3, fried	100
Size 4, raw	75
Size 4, fried	95
Size 5, raw	70
Size 5, fried	90
Yolk of size 3 egg, raw	65
White of size 3 egg, raw	15

Cheese
per 25g (1 oz) unless otherwise stated

Austrian Smoked	78
Blue Stilton	131
Boursin	116
Brie	88
Caerphilly	120
Camembert	88
Cheddar	120
Cheese Spread, per average triangle, 15g (¹/₂ oz)	40
Cheese Spread, per 15ml (1 level tablespoon)	50
Cheshire	110
Cotswold	105
Cottage cheese	125
Cottage cheese, per 15ml (1 level tablespoon)	15
Cream cheese	125
Cream cheese, per 15ml (1 level tablespoon)	60
Curd cheese	40
Curd cheese, per 15ml (1 level tablespoon)	20
Danish Blue	103
Danish Havarti	117
Danish Samsoe	98
Derby	110
Dolcellata	100
Double Gloucester	105
Edam	88
Fetta	54

Gouda	100
Gruyère	132
Jarlsberg	95
Lancashire	109
Leicester	105
Orangerulle	92
Parmesan	118
Parmesan, per 15ml (1 level tablespoon)	30
Philadelphia	90
Port Salut	94
Processed	88
Processed, Kraft Cheddar Singles Slice, each	65
Red Windsor	119
Riccotta	55
Sage Derby	112
Skimmed milk soft cheese	25
St Paulin	98
Wensleydale	115

Breakfast Cereals
per 25g (1 oz) unless otherwise stated

All Bran	70
30% Bran Flakes	90
Cornflakes	100
Frosties	100
Instant Porridge Oats	115
Muesli	105
Muesli, per 15ml (1 level tablespoon)	30
Rice Krispies *or* Ricicles	100
Shredded Wheat, each	80
Special K	100
Sugar Puffs	105
Sultana Bran	90
Weetabix, each	55

Bread and Bread Products

Bagel, 40g (1³/₈ oz)	150
Bran Bread, per small slice, 25g (1 oz)	65
Breadcrumbs, fresh, per 15ml (1 level tablespoon)	8
Breadcrumbs, dried, per 15ml (1 level tablespoon)	30
Bread stick, each	15
Brown *or* Wheatmeal Bread, per 25g (1 oz)	63
Croissant, small, 40g (1¹/₂ oz)	165
Croissant, large, 70g (2¹/₂ oz)	280
Crumpet, each	75
Crusty Roll, brown *or* white, 45g (1³/₄ oz)	145
Currant Bun, each	150
French Bread, per piece, 50g (2 oz)	130
Granary Bread, per small slice, 25g (1 oz)	70
Pitta Bread, per piece, 70g (2¹/₂ oz)	205
Soft Brown Roll, 45g (1³/₄ oz)	140
Soft White Roll, 45g (1³/₄ oz)	155
Wheatgerm Bread, per small slice, 25g (1 oz)	65
White Bread, per small slice, 25g (1 oz)	66
Wholemeal Bread, per small slice, 25g (1 oz)	61
Wholemeal roll, 45g (1³/₄ oz)	125

Pasta and Rice

Pasta, all shapes including lasagne, macaroni and spaghetti, raw, per 25g (1 oz)	105
Pasta, all shapes including lasagne, macaroni, and spaghetti, boiled, per 25g (1 oz)	33
Pasta, wholewheat, all shapes including lasagne, macaroni and spaghetti, raw, per 25g (1 oz)	95
Spaghetti, canned in tomato sauce, per 25g (1 oz)	17
Rice, brown, raw, per 25g (1 oz)	95
Rice, white, raw, per 25g (1 oz)	103
Rice, boiled, per 25g (1 oz)	35

Nuts

Almonds, shelled, per 25g (1 oz)	160
Almonds, whole, each	10
Brazil nuts, shelled, per 25g (1 oz)	176
Brazil nuts, each	20
Chocolate brazil, each	55
Cashew nuts, each	15
Cashew nuts, shelled, per 25g (1 oz)	160
Chestnuts, shelled, per 25g (1 oz)	48
Chestnuts, with shells, per 25g (1 oz)	40
Coconut, desiccated, per 15ml (1 level tablespoon)	30
Hazelnuts, shelled, per 25g (1 oz)	108
Hazelnuts, each	5
Mixed chopped nuts, per 15ml (1 level tablespoon)	30
Peanuts, dry roasted, per 25g (1 oz)	160
Peanuts, roasted and salted, per 25g (1 oz)	168
Walnuts, shelled, per 25g (1 oz)	149
Walnut, per walnut half	15

Milk
per 15ml (1 tablespoon)

Channel Island *or* Gold Top	15
Condensed, full cream, sweetened	50
Condensed, skimmed, sweetened	40
Evaporated	23
Homogenized, Pasteurized, Silver Top and Sterilized	10
Instant low-fat milk, dry	18
Instant low-fat milk, reconstituted	5
Skimmed *or* Separated	5

Milk
per 568ml (1 pint)

Channel Island *or* Gold Top	432
Evaporated milk, full cream reconstituted	360
Homogenized *or* Red Top	370
Instant spray dried low-fat skimmed milk, reconstituted	200

Instant dried skimmed milk with vegetable fat, reconstituted	280
Longlife *or* UHT	370
Pasteurized *or* Silver Top	370
Pasteurized *or* Silver Top with cream removed, 18 fl. oz (510ml)	240
Skimmed *or* Separated	200
Sterilized	370

Cream
per 15ml (1 level tablespoon)

Clotted	105
Double	60
Half	20
Imitation	55
Single	30
Soured	30
Sterilized, canned	35
Whipping	45

Fats
per 28g (1 oz)

Butter, all brands	210
Margarine, all brands except those labelled 'low-fat'	210
Low-fat Spread, all brands, e.g., Outline, St Ivel Gold, etc.	105

per 15ml (1 level tablespoon)

Butter *or* Margarine	105
Cooking *or* Salad Oil	120
Low-fat spread	50

per 5ml (1 level teaspoon)

Low-fat spread	15
Butter *or* margarine	35
Cooking *or* Salad Oil	40

Biscuits
per average biscuit

Chocolate Chip Cookie	60
Digestive, large	70
Digestive, medium	55
Digestive, small	45
Fig Roll	65
Garibaldi, per finger	30
Ginger Nut	40
Ginger Snap	35
Jaffa Cake	50
Lincoln	40
Malted Milk	40
Marie	30
Morning Coffee	25
Nice	45
Rich Osborne	35
Rich Tea Finger	25
Rich Tea Round	45
Sponge Finger	20
Thin Arrowroot	30

Sauces and Pickles
per 15ml (1 level tablespoon) unless otherwise stated

Apple Sauce, sweetened	20
Apple Sauce, unsweetened	10
Branston-type Pickle	20
Bread Sauce	15
Brown Sauce, bottled	15
Cranberry Jelly	50
Cranberry Sauce	45
French Dressing	75
Gherkins, per 25g (1 oz)	5
Horseradish Sauce	15
Low-calorie Oil-Free French Dressing	3
Low-calorie Salad Cream	25
Low-calorie Seafood Sauce	20

Low-calorie Tartare Sauce	25
Mango Chutney	35
Mayonnaise	95
Mint Sauce, diluted	5
Mustard, per 5ml (1 level teaspoon)	10
Olives, stuffed, per 25g (1 oz)	15
Piccalilli	10
Ploughmans Pickle	20
Redcurrant Jelly	45
Salad Cream	50
Soy Sauce	13
Sweet Pickle	20
Tartare Sauce	35
Tomato Ketchup	15
Vinegar	1
Worcestershire Sauce	13

Sugar, Jams and Marmalade
per 5ml (1 level teaspoon)

Sugar	17
Honey	18
Jam	17
Lemon Curd	13
Marmalade	17

DRINKS

Alcoholic Drinks

Wines

WHITE WINES

	Calories per 125ml 4 fl. oz glass	Calories per bottle
Bereich Nierstein	70	445
Bordeaux Blanc	80	490
Chablis	75	465
Crown of Crowns	70	445
Graves	85	515
Liebfraumilch	70	445
Mâcon Blanc	80	465
Moselle	70	420
Moselleblumchen	70	420
Piesporter Michelsburg	70	420
Riesling	75	465
Sauterne	100	615
SPARKLING WINES		
Asti Spumante	95	635
Champagne	85	555
ROSÉ WINES		
Anjou Rosé	80	490
Mateus Rosé	105	685
RED WINES		
Beaujolais	80	490
Claret	75	465
Côtes-du-Rhône	80	490
Médoc	75	465

Calorie Charts

Apéritifs and Vermouths

per pub measure, 50ml (¹/₃ gill)	*Calories*
Campari	115
Cinzano Bianco	80
Cinzano Rosso	75
Dubonnet Dry	55
Dubonnet Red	75
Fratelli Bianco Vermouth	75
Martini Bianco	75
Martini Extra Dry	55
Martini Rosso	80
Noilly Dry French	55
per pub measure 25ml (¹/₆ gill)	
Ouzo	60
Pernod	65

Sherry	*Calories*
per small schooner, 50ml (¹/₃ gill)	
Dry sherry	55
Medium Sherry	60
Sweet *or* Cream Sherry	65

Port	*Calories*
per pub measure, 50ml (¹/₃ gill)	
Average value for all ports	75

Liqueurs	*Calories*
per pub measure, 25ml (¹/₆ gill)	
Advocaat	60
Baileys Original Irish Cream	85
Benedictine	90
Calvados	60
Chartreuse (Green)	100
Cherry Brandy	65
Cointreau	85

Crème de Menthe	80
Drambuie	85
Galliano	75
Grand Marnier	80
Kirsch	50
Kummel	75
Sisca Crème de Cassis	65
Strega	75
Tia Maria	75

Other Drinks *Calories*
per individual standard bottle

Babycham Dry	60
Babycham Sweet	75
Cherry B	130
Crocodillo	60
Goldwell's Calypso	100
Goldwell's Wee McGlen	100
Moussec	95
Pony	115
Snowball	80

Lagers *Calories*
per 275ml (1/2 pint) unless otherwise stated

Arctic Lite Lager	80
Carling Black Label	85
Carlsberg Special Brew	205
Harp	80
Heineken	85
Hemeling	75
Holstein Pils Diabetic Lager, per 270ml (9½ fl. oz)	105
Lamot Pilsor Strong Lager, per 250ml (8.8 fl. oz)	110
Carlsberg Pilsner Lager	75
Skol	90
Stella Artois	120

Calorie Charts

Non-Alcoholic Lagers	Calories
Barbican, per 275ml (9.68 fl. oz)	45
Danish Light, per 320ml (11 fl. oz)	55

Spirits	Calories
per single pub measure 25ml (1/6 gill)	
Brandy, Gin, Rum, Whisky (Scotch, Irish *or* Bourbon) and Vodka	50
Southern Comfort	80

Ciders	Calories
per 285ml (1/2 pint)	

BULMERS

Bulmers No 7	100
Pomagne, Dry	140
Pomagne, Sweet	185
Special Reserve, Dry	130
Strongbow, draught	100
Strongbow, bottle	105
Woodpecker	80
Woodpecker, dry	85

GAYMERS

Festival Vat	130
Norfolk Dry	105
Olde English	115
Somerset	85
Triple Vintage	180

TAUNTON

Autumn Gold	90
Dry Blackthorn	120
Special Vat	135

Non-alcoholic Drinks

While you are dieting there is really no point in wasting calories on sweetened soft drinks. So we don't list them below. There are many low-calorie soft drinks easily available and they are all very acceptable alternatives to the high-calorie versions. Mineral waters, both still and carbonated, are calorie-free and can be drunk in as large a quantity as you wish. There is absolutely no need to restrict low-calorie and no-calorie fluids on a diet. Mineral water can bring a sparkle to a glass of wine and bring down its calories by half! Instead of your normal glass of wine, mix half wine with half mineral water. If you like to drink fresh fruit juices, you can also cut down your calories per glass by mixing them with mineral water – very refreshing.

	Calories
Mineral Water or Soda Water, all brands	0
BOOTS	
per 325-ml (11¹/₂-fl. oz) can	
Bitter Lemon *or* Lemonade	0
Cola, Orangeade *or* Lemon and Lime	5
BRITVIC	
Slimsta, Low-calorie range per 113-ml (4-fl. oz) bottle	
All varieties	0
CANADA DRY	
Low-calorie range, per 113-ml (4-fl. oz) bottle	
All varieties	0
CLUB	
per 185-ml (6¹/₂-fl. oz) bottle	
Low-calorie Bitter Lemon Drink	0
Low-calorie Orange Drink	5

Index